The Customer Equation : Building Connections + Driving Success

Vipresh Dwivedi

DEDICATION

I dedicate this book to my amazing team mates, whose dedication, collaboration, and unwavering support have been instrumental in shaping my understanding of customer service. Your commitment to excellence and passion for delivering exceptional experiences have inspired me throughout this journey. I also dedicate this book to all the students aspiring to build a career in the customer service industry. May this book serve as a guide and empower you to navigate the complexities of customer relationships with confidence and success.

Contents

ACKNOWLEDGMENTS

I WOULD LIKE TO EXPRESS MY HEARTFELT GRATITUDE TO THE SENIORS OF MY CURRENT AND PREVIOUS ORGANIZATIONS. YOUR GUIDANCE, SUPPORT, AND WISDOM HAVE BEEN INVALUABLE IN SHAPING MY UNDERSTANDING OF DEEP AND INTANGIBLE CUSTOMER MANAGEMENT STRATEGIES. YOUR MENTORSHIP HAS NOT ONLY ENABLED ME TO NAVIGATE COMPLEX CHALLENGES AND RESOLVE ISSUES, BUT IT HAS ALSO EMPOWERED ME TO BUILD STRONG AND MEANINGFUL RELATIONSHIPS WITH CUSTOMERS. I AM TRULY GRATEFUL FOR THE OPPORTUNITIES TO LEARN FROM YOUR EXPERTISE AND EXPERIENCE.

Preface

Welcome to " **The customer equation: Building Connections + Driving Success"** In today's highly competitive business landscape, the success of organizations hinges on their ability to cultivate meaningful relationships with customers. This comprehensive guide delves into the strategies, principles, and practices that empower businesses to achieve customer-centric excellence.

As you journey through the chapters of this book, you will gain invaluable insights into the importance of customer relationships, understanding customer needs and expectations, mapping the customer journey, effective customer communication, delivering exceptional customer experiences, building trust and loyalty, customer success strategies, building customer advocacy, continuous improvement, and much more.

Each chapter offers practical advice, real-world examples, and actionable strategies to help you transform your approach to customer relationships. Whether you are a business owner, a customer service professional, a sales executive, or a marketing specialist, this book provides you with the tools and knowledge needed to build strong connections with customers and ensure their success.

Drawing upon industry best practices and the latest research in customer relationship management, this guide will help you foster customer loyalty, drive revenue growth, and create a customer-centric organizational culture. You will discover how to leverage technology, implement personalized marketing campaigns, handle complaints effectively, measure customer satisfaction, and adapt to the ever-evolving needs and expectations of customers.

I would like to express my gratitude to the professionals and experts in the field of customer relationship management who have contributed their insights and expertise to make this book a comprehensive resource. Their collective wisdom and experiences have shaped the content and ensured its relevance and practicality.

I also want to extend my deepest appreciation to the readers of this book. It is your desire to enhance customer relationships and achieve customer success that has inspired me to share this knowledge with you. I hope that the strategies and principles outlined in this book will empower you to cultivate strong customer connections, drive business growth, and create remarkable customer experiences.

Let us embark on this journey together and unlock the potential of customer relationships in driving sustainable business success.

Best regards,

Vipresh Dwivedi

Chapter 1: The Importance of Customer Relationships

In this chapter, we explore the fundamental role that customer relationships play in the success of businesses. We delve into the significance of cultivating strong connections with customers and the impact it has on long-term loyalty and advocacy. By understanding the power of positive customer experiences, businesses can unlock the potential for repeat business and referrals. We discuss the importance of building a customer-centric organizational culture that prioritizes customer satisfaction and retention. Through real-life examples and case studies, we highlight the tangible benefits that businesses can gain by investing in customer relationships. This chapter sets the stage for the rest of the book, emphasizing the critical nature of fostering meaningful connections with customers in today's competitive business landscape.

- Recognizing the value of customer relationships in business success

Building strong and meaningful relationships with customers is essential for achieving long-term business success. In this section, we delve into the immense value that customer relationships bring to organizations. We explore how these relationships act as a foundation for customer loyalty, advocacy, and ultimately, business growth.

Firstly, recognizing the value of customer relationships involves understanding that customers are not just one-time transactions, but rather ongoing partners in the success of a business. By nurturing these relationships, organizations can create a loyal customer base that repeatedly chooses their products or services over competitors. Customer loyalty is a powerful asset that can lead to increased sales, higher profit margins, and a sustainable competitive advantage.

Additionally, customer relationships serve as a source of valuable feedback and insights. Engaging with customers allows businesses to gain a deep understanding of their needs, preferences, and pain points. This knowledge can then be utilized to improve products, enhance customer experiences, and tailor offerings to meet customer expectations. By actively listening to customers and incorporating their feedback into decision-making processes, organizations can stay ahead of the curve and continuously adapt to changing market dynamics.

Moreover, customer relationships contribute to positive word-of-mouth marketing. Satisfied customers are more likely to share their positive experiences with others, leading to increased brand visibility and reputation. This organic promotion can have a significant impact on attracting new customers and expanding the customer base.

Beyond financial benefits, strong customer relationships foster trust and loyalty. Customers who feel valued and appreciated are more likely to remain loyal, even when faced with competing offers. By investing in building relationships based on trust, organizations can create a customer-centric culture that prioritizes customer satisfaction and retention.

Finally, recognizing the value of customer relationships involves understanding that customers are not just revenue sources but individuals with unique needs and expectations. Treating customers as valued partners fosters a sense of connection and emotional attachment. When customers feel understood and cared for, they are more likely to develop a deep loyalty to a brand and become advocates, promoting the business through their personal networks.

The value of customer relationships in business success cannot be overstated. It is essential for organizations to recognize the intrinsic worth of these relationships, beyond immediate financial gains. By prioritizing customer satisfaction, actively engaging with customers, and fostering meaningful connections, businesses can cultivate loyalty, advocacy, and sustainable growth.

- Understanding the impact of positive customer experiences on loyalty and advocacy

Understanding the impact of positive customer experiences on loyalty and advocacy is crucial for businesses aiming to build strong, long-lasting relationships with their customers. When customers have positive experiences with a brand, it creates a ripple effect that extends beyond the initial transaction.

Positive customer experiences have a profound impact on customer loyalty. When customers have a seamless, enjoyable experience with a brand, they are more likely to become repeat customers. They develop a sense of trust and satisfaction, knowing that the brand consistently delivers on its promises. Loyal customers not only continue to purchase from the brand but also become advocates, sharing their positive experiences with others. They recommend the brand to friends, family, and colleagues, thereby increasing its visibility and attracting new customers.

Customer advocacy is a powerful marketing tool. Satisfied customers who become advocates create a ripple effect of positive word-of-mouth marketing. Their recommendations hold significant weight and influence the decisions of potential customers. This organic promotion can lead to increased brand awareness and a broader customer base. Moreover, customer advocates often go above and beyond by providing testimonials, participating in case studies, or sharing their experiences on social media. Their active support can significantly enhance a brand's reputation and credibility.

Positive customer experiences also foster customer loyalty in the face of competition. When customers have a memorable and satisfying experience, they are less likely to be swayed by competitors' offerings. They develop an emotional connection with the brand and feel a sense of loyalty, choosing to stick with the brand even when faced with alternatives. This loyalty acts as a buffer against the influence of price fluctuations or promotional activities by competitors.

Furthermore, positive customer experiences contribute to customer retention. When customers consistently have positive interactions with a brand, they are more likely to continue their relationship with the brand over the long term. This reduces customer churn and the need for expensive acquisition efforts to replace lost customers. Retaining existing customers is not only cost-effective but also allows businesses to focus on providing exceptional experiences and cultivating loyalty.

Understanding the impact of positive customer experiences on loyalty and advocacy is paramount for businesses. Positive experiences create loyal customers who become advocates, driving organic growth through word-of-mouth marketing. By prioritizing the delivery of exceptional customer experiences, businesses can cultivate loyalty, retain customers, and benefit from the positive ripple effect that spreads through advocacy and recommendations.

•Exploring the role of customer relationships in driving revenue and growth

Exploring the role of customer relationships in driving revenue and growth is essential for businesses seeking sustainable success. Customer relationships are not merely transactional; they play a crucial role in the overall financial performance and expansion of a business.

Firstly, strong customer relationships contribute to revenue growth by increasing customer retention. When businesses establish meaningful connections with their customers, it fosters loyalty and encourages repeat purchases. Loyal customers are more likely to continue engaging with a brand, leading to a consistent revenue stream. Moreover, satisfied customers are more open to upselling and cross-selling opportunities, which can further boost revenue generation.

Secondly, customer relationships have a significant impact on customer acquisition. Satisfied customers who have positive experiences with a brand often become brand advocates and refer others to the business. These referrals can be a powerful source of new customers, reducing the need for extensive marketing efforts and associated costs. Leveraging existing customer relationships to drive customer acquisition is not only cost-effective but also tends to yield high-quality leads with a greater likelihood of conversion.

Thirdly, customer relationships contribute to long-term business growth. By establishing strong relationships with their customers, businesses can gain valuable insights and feedback. This customer intelligence helps in identifying market trends, understanding evolving customer needs, and staying ahead of the competition. Businesses can leverage this information to innovate their products and services, ensuring continued relevance and appeal to their target audience. Additionally, satisfied customers are more likely to provide testimonials and positive reviews, which can enhance brand reputation and attract new customers.

Furthermore, customer relationships play a crucial role in fostering customer lifetime value (CLV). CLV refers to the total revenue a customer generates over their entire relationship with a business. By cultivating strong relationships, businesses can increase customer loyalty, drive repeat purchases, and extend the duration of the customer's engagement. This, in turn, leads to higher CLV, as customers continue to contribute to revenue over an extended period.

Exploring the role of customer relationships in driving

revenue and growth is vital for businesses. Strong customer relationships contribute to revenue growth through increased customer retention, customer acquisition through referrals, and long-term business growth through customer insights and innovation. By prioritizing the development and nurturing of customer relationships, businesses can create a solid foundation for sustainable revenue generation and overall business success.

• Building a customer-centric organizational culture

Building a customer-centric organizational culture is crucial for businesses aiming to prioritize customer satisfaction and deliver exceptional experiences. It involves aligning the values, mindset, and behaviors of employees with the goal of putting the customer at the center of everything the organization does.

A customer-centric organizational culture starts with leadership. Leaders play a vital role in setting the tone and creating an environment that fosters a customer-focused mindset. They must communicate the importance of customer-centricity and consistently reinforce it through their actions and decisions.

To build a customer-centric culture, organizations need to emphasize the value of customer feedback and actively seek input from customers. This involves establishing channels for feedback, such as surveys, customer interviews, and social media listening. By collecting and analyzing customer feedback, businesses can identify areas for improvement and make informed decisions that align with customer needs and expectations.

Employee empowerment is another key aspect of a customer-centric culture. Empowered employees have the autonomy and authority to make decisions that benefit the customer. This requires providing employees with the necessary tools, resources, and training to address customer concerns effectively. Organizations can also foster a culture of continuous learning and development, equipping employees with the skills and knowledge needed to deliver exceptional customer experiences.

Collaboration across departments is essential for creating a customer-centric culture. Silos and departmental boundaries can hinder effective customer service. By encouraging cross-functional collaboration and breaking down barriers, organizations can ensure a seamless and consistent customer experience throughout the customer journey. This involves facilitating communication, sharing customer insights and data, and aligning goals and objectives across departments.

Recognizing and rewarding customer-centric behaviors is crucial for reinforcing the desired culture. Organizations can implement reward and recognition programs that celebrate employees who consistently prioritize the customer. This encourages employees to go above and beyond in delivering exceptional experiences and reinforces the organization's commitment to customer satisfaction.

Lastly, a customer-centric culture requires a focus on continuous improvement. Organizations should foster a mindset of innovation and adaptability, encouraging employees to explore new ideas and approaches to meet evolving customer needs. This involves regularly evaluating processes, systems, and policies to identify areas for improvement and make necessary changes.

Building a customer-centric organizational culture is a strategic imperative for businesses. It involves leadership commitment, employee empowerment, collaboration, continuous learning, and a focus on customer feedback and improvement. By fostering a customer-centric culture, organizations can differentiate themselves in the market, build long-term customer relationships, and drive sustainable business growth.

Chapter 2: Understanding Customer Needs and Expectations

In this chapter, we delve into the critical aspect of comprehending what customers truly desire from businesses. We explore the importance of conducting market research to identify customer demographics and preferences, pinpointing pain points and challenges faced by customers, defining customer personas and segments, and staying attuned to evolving customer expectations. By gaining a deep understanding of customer needs and expectations, organizations can tailor their products, services, and experiences to meet those demands effectively, ensuring customer satisfaction and loyalty. This chapter equips businesses with the insights and tools necessary to align their offerings with customer desires and deliver exceptional value.

- Conducting market research to understand customer demographics and preferences

Understanding customer demographics and preferences is a crucial aspect of building successful businesses.

Conducting comprehensive market research allows organizations to gather valuable insights about their target audience. By analyzing demographic data such as age, gender, location, and income levels, businesses can gain a deeper understanding of their customers' characteristics and preferences.

Market research also helps identify customer preferences by studying their buying behavior, interests, and needs. This involves conducting surveys, interviews, and focus groups to collect data directly from customers. By analyzing this data, businesses can identify patterns and trends that inform their marketing strategies and product development.

Another key aspect of market research is competitor analysis. By studying the strategies, strengths, and weaknesses of competitors, businesses can identify opportunities to differentiate themselves in the market. This includes analyzing competitor products, pricing, distribution channels, and marketing campaigns.

Moreover, market research helps businesses stay updated with the latest industry trends and changes. By monitoring market dynamics, emerging technologies, and consumer behavior shifts, organizations can adapt their strategies to meet evolving customer demands.

Conducting market research involves both quantitative and qualitative methods. Quantitative research involves collecting and analyzing numerical data, such as surveys with closed-ended questions, while qualitative research involves gathering subjective insights through interviews and open-ended questions. Both approaches provide valuable information that helps businesses make informed decisions.

Overall, conducting market research is essential for understanding customer demographics and preferences. It enables businesses to tailor their products, services, and marketing efforts to meet customer expectations effectively. By staying attuned to customer needs, businesses can develop stronger customer relationships, drive customer loyalty, and gain a competitive edge in the market.

- Identifying customer pain points and challenges

Identifying customer pain points and challenges is a critical aspect of understanding customers' needs and improving their overall experience. It involves recognizing the areas where customers face difficulties, frustrations, or unmet needs in relation to a product or service.

One effective way to identify customer pain points is through feedback collection. This can be done through various channels such as surveys, customer support interactions, online reviews, and social media monitoring. By actively listening to customer feedback and analyzing their comments, businesses can gain valuable insights into the specific pain points they encounter.

Additionally, businesses can conduct in-depth interviews or focus groups with customers to delve deeper into their challenges. These qualitative research methods provide an opportunity to understand customers' experiences and uncover pain points that may not be apparent through quantitative data alone.

Another approach to identifying customer pain points is by analyzing customer behavior and engagement data. By studying customer interactions with a website, app, or product, businesses can identify patterns or bottlenecks that may cause frustration or dissatisfaction. For example, high bounce rates, abandoned shopping carts, or low engagement in certain features may indicate areas of concern.

Customer pain points can also be discovered through competitor analysis. By studying competitors' offerings and customer reviews, businesses can identify gaps in the market and areas where they can provide a better solution or address unmet needs.

Once customer pain points are identified, businesses can prioritize them based on their impact and frequency. This allows them to focus on resolving the most critical pain points that have the potential to significantly enhance the customer experience.

By addressing customer pain points, businesses can improve customer satisfaction, loyalty, and retention. It enables them to develop innovative solutions and strategies that alleviate customer frustrations and meet their expectations more effectively.

Ultimately, the process of identifying customer pain points is an ongoing endeavor as customer needs and challenges evolve over time. By continuously listening to customer feedback, monitoring behavior, and staying attuned to industry trends, businesses can proactively address pain points and deliver exceptional customer experiences.

•Defining customer personas and segmenting the target audience

Defining customer personas and segmenting the target audience is a crucial step in understanding the diverse needs, preferences, and behaviors of customers. It involves creating fictional representations of different customer types or profiles based on common characteristics, demographics, and psychographics.

To define customer personas, businesses gather data from various sources such as market research, surveys, interviews, and customer feedback. This information helps in identifying patterns and trends that can be used to develop distinct personas. These personas typically include details such as age, gender, occupation, interests, goals, challenges, and buying behaviors.

Segmenting the target audience involves dividing the overall customer base into smaller, more manageable groups based on specific criteria. This segmentation can be done using variables like demographics (age, gender, location), psychographics (values, attitudes, interests), behavior (purchasing patterns, usage frequency), or firmographics (company size, industry). Each segment represents a distinct subset of customers with similar characteristics and needs.

Defining customer personas and segmenting the target audience offers several benefits. It allows businesses to:

1. Gain a deeper understanding of customers: By creating detailed personas, businesses can develop empathy and a better understanding of the motivations, desires, and pain points of different customer segments. This understanding helps in tailoring products, services, and marketing efforts to meet their specific needs.

2. Improve marketing and messaging: Customer personas and audience segments enable businesses to create targeted marketing campaigns and messaging. By understanding the preferences, interests, and communication channels preferred by each segment,

businesses can deliver personalized and relevant content that resonates with their audience.

3. Enhance product development: Customer segmentation provides insights into the specific needs and preferences of different customer groups. This information can guide product development efforts, ensuring that new offerings address the unique requirements of each segment. It helps in creating products that cater to specific market niches and have a higher chance of success.

4. Optimize customer experience: By understanding the different customer personas and segments, businesses can tailor the customer experience to meet their specific expectations. This includes designing user interfaces, customer support processes, and touchpoints that align with the preferences and behaviors of each segment.

Overall, defining customer personas and segmenting the target audience enables businesses to develop a more customer-centric approach. It helps in delivering personalized experiences, effective marketing strategies, and tailored products and services that cater to the diverse needs of customers. By understanding the nuances of each segment, businesses can build stronger relationships, increase customer satisfaction, and drive business growth.

•Anticipating and addressing evolving customer expectations

Anticipating and addressing evolving customer expectations is a critical aspect of building successful customer relationships. As customer preferences and needs constantly evolve, businesses must stay proactive in understanding and meeting these changing expectations.

To anticipate evolving customer expectations, businesses must closely monitor industry trends, market research, and customer feedback. This involves keeping a pulse on emerging technologies, social and cultural shifts, and competitor offerings that may impact customer expectations. By staying informed and up-to-date, businesses can anticipate potential changes in customer demands and preferences.

Addressing evolving customer expectations requires businesses to be agile and responsive. This involves:

1. **Continuous learning:** Businesses should invest in ongoing learning and development to stay updated with industry trends and customer needs. This includes attending conferences, participating in industry forums, and engaging in continuous education to acquire the knowledge and skills needed to meet evolving expectations.

2. **Active listening:** By actively listening to customer feedback and engaging in open and honest communication, businesses can gain valuable insights into changing expectations. This can be done through surveys, focus groups, customer support interactions, and social media monitoring. By capturing customer feedback, businesses can identify areas for improvement and make necessary adjustments.

3. **Innovation and adaptation:** Businesses should foster a culture of innovation and be willing to adapt their products, services, and processes to align with evolving customer expectations. This

may involve investing in new technologies, redesigning user experiences, or introducing new features that address emerging customer needs.

4. **Personalization:** As customer expectations shift towards more personalized experiences, businesses should strive to deliver tailored offerings. This can include personalized marketing campaigns, customized product recommendations, and personalized customer support interactions. By treating customers as individuals and catering to their unique preferences, businesses can create memorable experiences that exceed expectations.

5. **Continuous improvement:** Businesses should embrace a mindset of continuous improvement and actively seek ways to enhance their offerings. This can involve soliciting feedback, conducting regular performance evaluations, and benchmarking against industry standards. By striving for excellence and constantly evolving, businesses can ensure they are meeting and surpassing customer expectations.

By anticipating and addressing evolving customer expectations, businesses can differentiate themselves in the market and build long-lasting customer relationships. It requires a commitment to understanding customer needs, staying adaptable, and continuously improving to meet the changing demands of the market. Ultimately, businesses that successfully navigate and exceed evolving customer expectations are more likely to thrive in today's dynamic business landscape.

Chapter 3: Mapping the Customer Journey

This chapter, delves into the process of understanding and mapping the customer journey to create exceptional experiences. This chapter explores how businesses can identify key touchpoints, moments of truth, and customer emotions throughout the journey. It emphasizes the importance of designing seamless and personalized experiences at each stage and leveraging data and analytics to optimize the customer journey. By gaining insights into the customer's perspective, businesses can deliver targeted and impactful interactions, ultimately leading to increased customer satisfaction, loyalty, and advocacy.

- Mapping the customer journey to identify touchpoints and interactions

Mapping the customer journey is a critical process in understanding the various stages and touchpoints that customers go through when interacting with a business. By mapping the customer journey, businesses can gain valuable insights into the customer's experience, identify pain points, and optimize interactions.

The first step in mapping the customer journey is to identify the touchpoints, which are the points of contact between the customer and the business. These touchpoints can include visiting a website, making a purchase, contacting customer support, or receiving post-purchase emails. By identifying these touchpoints, businesses can gain a comprehensive view of the customer's interactions with the brand.

Once the touchpoints are identified, it is essential to analyze the customer's experience at each touchpoint. This involves understanding the customer's expectations, needs, and emotions during those interactions. It is important to consider both positive and negative experiences to gain a holistic understanding of the customer journey.

Mapping the customer journey also involves identifying key interactions between the customer and the business. These interactions can be both digital and physical, such as browsing a website, engaging on social media, attending events, or receiving product deliveries. By recognizing these interactions, businesses can focus on optimizing them to create a seamless and satisfying customer experience.

Through mapping the customer journey, businesses can identify pain points and areas for improvement. For example, if customers frequently abandon their shopping carts on the website, it indicates a potential issue in the checkout process. By addressing such pain points, businesses can enhance the customer experience and increase conversion rates.

Furthermore, mapping the customer journey helps businesses understand the customer's perspective and align their processes and strategies accordingly. By gaining insights into the customer's motivations, desires, and challenges at each stage, businesses can tailor their offerings, communications, and support to meet customer expectations.

Mapping the customer journey is a valuable exercise that allows businesses to identify touchpoints, analyze interactions, and uncover pain points. By understanding the customer's experience and perspective, businesses can optimize their processes, improve customer satisfaction, and drive long-term loyalty and advocacy.

•Identifying key moments of truth and customer emotions throughout the journey

Identifying key moments of truth and understanding customer emotions throughout their journey is crucial for businesses to create exceptional customer experiences. These moments of truth are critical touchpoints where customers form lasting impressions and make decisions about their relationship with a brand.

To identify key moments of truth, businesses must closely examine each stage of the customer journey and identify the interactions that significantly impact the customer's perception. These interactions can vary from the first website visit or initial contact to post-purchase support or ongoing engagement. By pinpointing these moments, businesses can allocate resources and focus their efforts on delivering exceptional experiences.

Customer emotions play a vital role in shaping their overall perception and loyalty towards a brand. Emotional responses can range from joy and satisfaction to frustration or disappointment. By understanding and tracking customer emotions at each touchpoint, businesses can gauge the effectiveness of their interactions and make necessary improvements. For example, if customers consistently feel frustrated during the onboarding process, it indicates the need to streamline and simplify that stage to enhance customer satisfaction.

Moreover, identifying customer emotions allows businesses to personalize their interactions and tailor experiences based on individual needs. For instance, if a customer expresses excitement about a new product launch, businesses can provide targeted content or exclusive offers to further nurture that positive emotion. By leveraging customer emotions, businesses can create meaningful connections and foster long-term loyalty.

It is essential to consider both positive and negative emotions throughout the customer journey. Positive emotions, such as delight or surprise, can strengthen the customer's connection with the brand, while negative emotions, if not addressed promptly, can lead to dissatisfaction and churn. By proactively managing customer emotions, businesses can turn negative experiences into positive ones and recover from potential setbacks.

By identifying key moments of truth and understanding customer emotions, businesses gain insights into critical touchpoints that significantly impact the customer's perception and overall experience. This knowledge empowers businesses to design targeted interventions, provide exceptional service, and create memorable moments that drive customer satisfaction, loyalty, and advocacy. Ultimately, the ability to identify and leverage these key moments is crucial for delivering exceptional customer experiences and building strong, lasting relationships with customers.

•Designing seamless and personalized experiences at each touchpoint

Designing seamless and personalized experiences at each touchpoint is vital for businesses to create exceptional customer journeys. It involves understanding customer preferences, needs, and behaviors to tailor interactions and deliver a cohesive experience across various channels.

To design seamless experiences, businesses must ensure smooth transitions between different touchpoints, eliminating any friction or obstacles that may hinder the customer's journey. This requires a holistic view of the customer's interactions, from the initial engagement to post-purchase support. By mapping out these touchpoints and identifying potential pain points or gaps, businesses can optimize processes and enhance the overall customer experience.

Personalization is a key aspect of designing exceptional experiences. It involves tailoring interactions and content based on individual customer preferences and characteristics. By leveraging customer data, businesses can gather insights that allow them to deliver relevant and targeted experiences. Personalization can take various forms, such as personalized recommendations, customized communication, or tailored offers. These personalized experiences create a sense of connection and make customers feel valued, ultimately fostering loyalty and satisfaction.

To achieve seamless and personalized experiences, businesses must leverage technology and data-driven insights. Advanced customer relationship management (CRM) systems, analytics tools, and automation technologies enable businesses to collect, analyze, and utilize customer data effectively. This data can provide valuable insights into customer preferences, behaviors, and patterns, enabling businesses to personalize interactions and deliver the right message at the right time.

Moreover, businesses should align their touchpoints and messaging across different channels to ensure consistency and coherence. This includes aligning the brand's voice, visual identity, and messaging across various digital platforms, physical stores, customer support channels, and marketing campaigns. Consistency in the customer experience enhances brand perception and fosters trust and familiarity.

Designing seamless and personalized experiences requires ongoing monitoring and optimization. By continuously gathering customer feedback, analyzing metrics, and testing new approaches, businesses can refine their touchpoints and fine-tune their strategies. This iterative process allows businesses to stay responsive to evolving customer expectations and deliver experiences that meet or exceed their needs.

Each touchpoint is crucial for creating exceptional customer journeys. It involves understanding customer preferences, leveraging technology and data, and ensuring consistency across channels. By focusing on these aspects, businesses can enhance customer satisfaction, foster loyalty, and differentiate themselves in a competitive marketplace.

•Leveraging data and analytics to optimize the customer journey

Leveraging data and analytics to optimize the customer journey is a crucial aspect of customer relationship management. By utilizing the vast amounts of data available, businesses can gain valuable insights into customer behavior, preferences, and pain points, allowing them to make data-driven decisions and deliver personalized experiences.

Data and analytics provide businesses with the opportunity to understand the customer journey in depth. Through the collection and analysis of various data points, including customer interactions, purchasing behavior, website navigation patterns, and social media engagements, businesses can gain a comprehensive view of the customer's journey. This allows them to identify bottlenecks, areas of improvement, and opportunities for enhanced engagement.

One of the key benefits of leveraging data and analytics

is the ability to personalize the customer journey. By understanding individual customer preferences and behaviors, businesses can tailor their marketing messages, product recommendations, and overall customer experiences. This personalization leads to increased customer satisfaction, as customers feel understood and valued by the brand.

Furthermore, data and analytics help businesses identify patterns and trends that can shape their strategies. By analyzing customer data, businesses can uncover insights about their target audience, such as demographic trends, purchasing habits, and product preferences. This information can inform marketing campaigns, product development, and overall business strategies, allowing businesses to align their offerings with customer needs and expectations.

Data-driven decision making also enables businesses to optimize the customer journey by identifying and addressing pain points. By analyzing customer feedback and behavior data, businesses can pinpoint areas where customers may face challenges or frustrations. Armed with this knowledge, businesses can take proactive measures to improve those touchpoints, enhance the overall customer experience, and reduce customer churn.

Moreover, leveraging data and analytics allows businesses to track and measure the effectiveness of their customer journey initiatives. Key performance indicators (KPIs) can be established to monitor the success of specific strategies and track the impact of changes made to the customer journey. By continuously analyzing data and monitoring KPIs, businesses can make data-driven adjustments and improvements to optimize the customer journey over time.

Leveraging data and analytics is essential for optimizing the customer journey. By harnessing the power of data, businesses can personalize experiences, identify pain points, uncover insights, and make data-driven decisions. This ultimately leads to enhanced customer satisfaction, increased loyalty, and improved business performance.

Chapter 4: Effective Customer Communication

This chapter, explores the crucial role of communication in building and maintaining strong customer relationships. This chapter delves into various aspects of customer communication, including developing a customer-centric communication strategy, tailoring communication channels to customer preferences, active listening and understanding customer feedback, and building trust and transparency through open and honest communication. By mastering effective customer communication, businesses can enhance customer satisfaction, foster stronger connections, and drive customer loyalty. Through practical tips and strategies, this chapter empowers businesses to communicate effectively with their customers, ensuring clear, meaningful, and impactful interactions at every touchpoint.

•Developing a customer-centric communication strategy

Developing a customer-centric communication strategy is vital for businesses aiming to establish strong and meaningful connections with their customers. It involves crafting an approach that places the customer at the center of all communication efforts. This strategy entails understanding the unique needs, preferences, and expectations of customers and tailoring communication accordingly. It involves selecting appropriate communication channels and methods that resonate with the target audience, such as email, social media, or in-person interactions.

To develop a customer-centric communication strategy, businesses must first conduct thorough research to understand their customers' demographics, communication preferences, and pain points. This data serves as a foundation for creating personalized and relevant messages that address customers' specific needs.

An effective customer-centric communication strategy also emphasizes the importance of active listening. It involves actively seeking customer feedback, understanding their concerns, and responding promptly and empathetically. By listening attentively to customers, businesses can gain valuable insights into their experiences, identify areas for improvement, and demonstrate that their opinions matter.

Building trust and transparency is another key aspect of a customer-centric communication strategy. Open and honest communication helps establish credibility and foster long-term relationships with customers. By being transparent about product features, pricing, and policies, businesses can build trust and loyalty among their customer base.

Moreover, a customer-centric communication strategy considers the value of personalization. It involves tailoring messages and experiences to individual customers, making them feel recognized and valued. Personalized communication can be achieved through techniques like segmentation, where customers are grouped based on shared characteristics or preferences, allowing for more targeted and relevant interactions.

Ultimately, developing a customer-centric communication strategy requires a deep understanding of customers and a commitment to meeting their needs and expectations. By putting customers at the forefront of communication efforts, businesses can enhance customer satisfaction, build trust and loyalty, and differentiate themselves in a competitive market.

•Tailoring communication channels to customer preferences

Tailoring communication channels to customer preferences is a crucial aspect of effective customer communication. In today's digital age, customers have diverse preferences when it comes to communication channels, and businesses need to adapt to meet their needs. By understanding and catering to these preferences, businesses can enhance customer engagement, satisfaction, and overall communication effectiveness.

To tailor communication channels, businesses must first gather information about their customers' preferred channels. This can be done through surveys, feedback forms, or by analyzing customer data. It's essential to consider factors such as age, demographics, and technological proficiency to determine the most suitable channels for each customer segment.

Once customer preferences are identified, businesses can utilize various communication channels such as email, phone calls, text messages, social media platforms, and mobile apps. Each channel has its unique strengths and offers different benefits. For example, email is ideal for longer, more detailed messages, while social media platforms are effective for quick updates and engaging with customers in real-time.

Moreover, personalization plays a significant role in tailoring communication channels. Businesses can use customer data to segment their audience and send targeted messages through the preferred channels of each segment. This approach ensures that customers receive information that is relevant to their needs, increasing the likelihood of engagement and response.

Additionally, businesses should also consider the accessibility and convenience of different channels. For example, offering self-service options through a user-friendly website or mobile app allows customers to access information and resolve issues at their convenience. This empowers customers and saves them time and effort, leading to higher satisfaction levels.

It's important to regularly review and adapt communication channels based on customer feedback and evolving trends. Technology and customer preferences change over time, and businesses need to stay updated to ensure their communication channels remain effective and relevant.

Tailoring communication channels to customer preferences is essential for successful customer communication. By understanding customer preferences, leveraging the appropriate channels, and personalizing communication, businesses can enhance engagement, build stronger relationships, and meet customer expectations effectively. This approach helps businesses stay connected with their customers and ensures a positive and seamless communication experience.

•Active listening and understanding customer feedback

Active listening and understanding customer feedback are vital components of effective customer communication. It involves attentively and empathetically listening to what customers have to say, interpreting their feedback, and taking appropriate actions based on their insights. By actively engaging with customers and valuing their feedback, businesses can foster stronger relationships, improve products and services, and enhance overall customer satisfaction.

Active listening begins with giving undivided attention to the customer. This means eliminating distractions, maintaining eye contact, and showing genuine interest in what they are saying. It also involves being present in the conversation and avoiding interruptions or jumping to conclusions. By actively listening, businesses can gain a deeper understanding of the customer's perspective, needs, and concerns.

Understanding customer feedback goes beyond simply hearing their words. It involves analyzing and interpreting their feedback to uncover valuable insights. This includes identifying common themes, trends, and patterns in customer feedback to gain a holistic understanding of their preferences and expectations. It also involves considering the emotional context behind the feedback and understanding the underlying motivations and sentiments expressed.

Businesses can employ various techniques to enhance their understanding of customer feedback. This may include using sentiment analysis tools to analyze the emotional tone of customer feedback or conducting surveys and interviews to gather more detailed insights. Additionally, businesses can leverage data analytics to identify correlations between customer feedback and specific business outcomes, enabling them to make data-driven decisions.

Once customer feedback is understood, businesses should take appropriate actions to address their concerns and improve their products, services, or processes. This may involve making necessary changes, implementing corrective measures, or initiating proactive communication to resolve issues and meet customer expectations. It's important to communicate with customers about the actions taken based on their feedback, demonstrating that their input is valued and acted upon.

Active listening and understanding customer feedback are crucial for effective customer communication. By attentively listening to customers, interpreting their feedback, and taking appropriate actions, businesses can enhance their understanding of customer needs, improve their offerings, and build stronger relationships. It's a continuous process that requires ongoing engagement and a customer-centric mindset to ensure that customer feedback is not only heard but also used to drive positive changes and deliver exceptional experiences.

•Building trust and transparency through open and honest communication

Building trust and transparency through open and honest communication is essential for fostering strong relationships with customers. When businesses prioritize transparency, they establish an environment of trust, which in turn enhances customer loyalty and satisfaction.

Open communication involves sharing information with customers in a clear and accessible manner. It means providing accurate and relevant details about products, services, pricing, and policies. Open communication also includes being proactive in addressing customer concerns, promptly responding to inquiries, and providing updates on any changes or developments that may impact customers.

Honesty is another critical aspect of building trust. It involves being truthful and forthcoming in all interactions with customers. This includes admitting mistakes or shortcomings and taking responsibility for them. When businesses are honest, customers perceive them as credible and reliable, which strengthens the foundation of trust.

Transparency goes beyond providing information; it also involves being open about business processes, practices, and values. This may include sharing the company's mission, vision, and ethical standards. Transparent businesses demonstrate accountability and integrity, ensuring that customers feel confident in their interactions and transactions.

Establishing trust and transparency requires effective communication strategies. Businesses should strive to be proactive in their communication efforts, anticipating customer needs and concerns, and addressing them proactively. This may involve providing comprehensive product information, offering clear terms and conditions, and setting realistic expectations. Additionally, businesses should actively seek and encourage customer feedback, demonstrating their commitment to improving customer experiences.

Trust is built over time through consistent and reliable communication. It is important to deliver on promises and meet or exceed customer expectations. By consistently demonstrating transparency and delivering what is communicated, businesses can reinforce the trust that customers have in their brand.

Open and honest communication also creates an environment where customers feel comfortable expressing their concerns, providing valuable feedback, and engaging in constructive dialogue. This enables businesses to identify areas for improvement and make necessary adjustments to meet customer needs effectively.

Building trust and transparency through open and honest communication is crucial for establishing strong and long-lasting customer relationships. By prioritizing clear and accessible communication, being honest and transparent in all interactions, and consistently delivering on promises, businesses can foster trust, enhance customer satisfaction, and differentiate themselves in the marketplace.

Chapter 5: Delivering Exceptional Customer Experiences

This chapter explores the strategies and practices required to provide outstanding customer experiences. It emphasizes the importance of designing and implementing customer experience strategies that go beyond meeting basic expectations. The chapter delves into the concept of personalization, emphasizing the need to tailor interactions and experiences to individual customer preferences. It also covers the effective resolution of customer issues and complaints, highlighting the significance of going above and beyond to exceed customer expectations. Additionally, the chapter emphasizes the importance of continuous improvement and innovation to consistently enhance customer experiences and maintain a competitive edge in the market.

- Designing and implementing customer experience strategies

Designing and implementing customer experience strategies is a crucial aspect of ensuring exceptional customer experiences. This involves creating a comprehensive plan to guide interactions and touchpoints throughout the customer journey. The strategy should align with the organization's overall goals and objectives, as well as the specific needs and preferences of the target customer base.

To begin, organizations must conduct thorough research and analysis to gain insights into customer expectations, pain points, and preferences. This information serves as the foundation for designing a customer experience strategy that addresses these needs effectively. The strategy should focus on delivering personalized and seamless experiences at every stage of the customer journey.

Key elements of designing a customer experience strategy include defining the desired customer experience, setting clear objectives, and identifying the necessary resources and capabilities. It also involves mapping out the customer journey to identify key touchpoints and interactions, ensuring a consistent and cohesive experience across channels and platforms.

Implementing the strategy requires collaboration and coordination across various departments and functions within the organization. It involves training employees to deliver exceptional customer service, providing them with the necessary tools and resources to fulfill customer needs. Regular communication and feedback loops are essential to track progress, identify areas for improvement, and make adjustments as needed.

Successful implementation of customer experience strategies goes beyond individual transactions. It involves creating an emotional connection with customers, building long-term relationships based on trust and loyalty. Organizations should continuously monitor customer feedback and leverage data and analytics to measure the effectiveness of their strategies and make data-driven improvements.

By designing and implementing effective customer experience strategies, organizations can differentiate themselves in the market and foster customer loyalty. This not only leads to increased customer satisfaction but also drives customer advocacy and positive word-of-mouth referrals. Ultimately, a well-executed customer experience strategy can contribute to business growth, profitability, and sustainable success.

• Personalizing customer interactions and tailoring experiences

Personalizing customer interactions and tailoring experiences is a key aspect of delivering exceptional customer service and building strong relationships. It involves understanding and catering to the unique needs, preferences, and characteristics of individual customers.

To personalize customer interactions, organizations need to gather relevant customer data and leverage it effectively. This includes information such as demographics, purchase history, browsing behavior, and preferences. By capturing and analyzing this data, organizations can gain insights into each customer's preferences, interests, and motivations.

With this information, organizations can customize their communication and engagement strategies. This may involve addressing customers by their names, offering personalized recommendations or product suggestions based on their past purchases, or tailoring marketing messages to align with their specific interests. By doing so, organizations can create a sense of personalization and make customers feel valued and understood.

Tailoring experiences goes beyond personalizing communication. It involves designing customer journeys and touchpoints that align with individual preferences and needs. This may include providing multiple channels for customer interaction, such as in-person, online, or mobile, allowing customers to choose their preferred mode of engagement. It also includes offering flexible options for delivery, payment, or support based on customer preferences.

Moreover, organizations can leverage technology to enhance personalization. This may involve implementing customer relationship management (CRM) systems, customer segmentation tools, or artificial intelligence (AI) algorithms to analyze customer data and deliver personalized experiences at scale. Chatbots, personalized recommendations, or customized product configurations are some examples of how technology can enable tailored experiences.

Personalizing customer interactions and tailoring experiences can have several benefits. It enhances customer satisfaction by meeting their specific needs and expectations, which leads to increased loyalty and repeat business. It also boosts customer engagement and drives higher conversion rates as customers feel more connected and valued by the organization. Additionally, personalized experiences generate positive word-of-mouth and referrals, attracting new customers to the brand.

Overall, personalizing customer interactions and tailoring experiences is a powerful strategy to create meaningful and lasting connections with customers. By treating each customer as an individual and providing tailored solutions, organizations can foster customer loyalty, drive customer success, and differentiate themselves in a competitive market.

•Resolving customer issues and handling complaints effectively

Resolving customer issues and handling complaints effectively is crucial for maintaining customer satisfaction and building strong relationships. Every business encounters customer complaints and problems at some point, and how these issues are addressed can significantly impact the overall customer experience.

To effectively resolve customer issues, businesses need to have a systematic approach in place. This involves:

1. **Prompt response:** Acknowledging and responding to customer complaints in a timely manner is essential. Customers appreciate quick acknowledgment and reassurance that their concerns are being addressed.

2. **Active listening:** Listening attentively to customers' concerns is vital to understand the issue fully. This includes asking clarifying questions, paraphrasing, and empathizing with their emotions. Active listening demonstrates that the business values the customer's perspective and is committed to finding a resolution.

3. **Problem analysis:** Conducting a thorough analysis of the problem helps in identifying the root cause and finding an appropriate solution. This may involve gathering additional information, consulting relevant teams or departments, and evaluating any potential gaps in processes or products.

4. **Empathetic communication:** Demonstrating

empathy and understanding towards customers' emotions is crucial. It reassures them that their concerns are being taken seriously and helps build rapport. Communicating with empathy involves using compassionate language, validating their feelings, and expressing genuine concern for their experience.

5. **Solutions-oriented approach:** Offering practical and viable solutions to resolve the issue is key. This may involve providing alternatives, offering refunds or replacements, or implementing corrective actions to prevent similar issues in the future. The goal is to find a solution that meets the customer's needs while aligning with the organization's capabilities.

6. **Follow-up and feedback:** After resolving the issue, following up with the customer to ensure their satisfaction is essential. This demonstrates commitment to their experience and provides an opportunity to gather feedback for further improvement.

Effective resolution of customer issues has several

benefits. It helps in retaining customers, as they feel valued and supported by the business. It also enhances the business's reputation and credibility, as positive experiences with issue resolution can lead to positive word-of-mouth referrals. Furthermore, it provides valuable insights into areas of improvement, allowing businesses to refine their processes and prevent similar issues in the future.

By focusing on resolving customer issues and handling complaints effectively, businesses can turn challenging situations into opportunities for building trust, loyalty, and long-term customer relationships.

•Continuously improving and innovating customer experiences

Continuously improving and innovating customer experiences is essential for businesses to stay competitive in today's dynamic marketplace. Customers' expectations are constantly evolving, and businesses need to adapt and innovate to meet those changing demands. By continuously improving and innovating customer experiences, businesses can foster customer loyalty, drive satisfaction, and differentiate themselves from their competitors.

To achieve continuous improvement and innovation in customer experiences, businesses can consider the following strategies:

1. **Collecting customer feedback:** Actively seeking and collecting customer feedback is crucial in identifying areas for improvement. This can be done through surveys, feedback forms, online reviews, or social media monitoring. Analyzing this feedback helps businesses gain insights into customer preferences, pain points, and areas that require improvement.

2. **Monitoring customer trends:** Keeping an eye on emerging customer trends and market dynamics is essential for staying ahead of the curve. By monitoring customer behavior, preferences, and expectations, businesses can identify opportunities for innovation and tailor their experiences to meet those evolving needs.

3. **Embracing technology:** Leveraging technology can greatly enhance customer experiences. Businesses can explore the use of emerging

technologies such as artificial intelligence, machine learning, chatbots, and personalized recommendation systems to provide more personalized and efficient experiences. Embracing technology enables businesses to automate processes, offer self-service options, and deliver seamless interactions across various channels.

4. **Cultivating a culture of innovation:** Fostering a culture of innovation within the organization is crucial for continuous improvement. Encouraging employees to think creatively, experiment with new ideas, and share insights can lead to innovative solutions and improved customer experiences. Providing resources and support for innovation initiatives can further fuel a culture of continuous improvement.

5. **Collaboration and partnerships:** Collaborating with customers, industry partners, and technology providers can bring fresh perspectives and enable businesses to tap into new opportunities. Partnerships can lead to joint innovation projects, knowledge sharing, and access to new technologies, ultimately benefiting the customer experience.

6. **Data-driven decision making:** Making informed decisions based on data and analytics is vital for continuous improvement. By analyzing customer data, businesses can identify patterns, trends, and areas of improvement. Data-driven insights enable businesses to make targeted improvements and measure the impact of those changes on customer experiences.

Continuous improvement and innovation in customer experiences are ongoing processes. By actively seeking feedback, monitoring trends, embracing technology, fostering a culture of innovation, and making data-driven decisions, businesses can ensure that they stay relevant and deliver exceptional customer experiences in a rapidly changing landscape. This commitment to continuous improvement fosters customer loyalty, drives customer satisfaction, and sets businesses apart from their competitors.

Chapter 6: Building Trust and Loyalty

This chapter explores the crucial aspects of establishing and nurturing trust-based relationships with customers. It delves into the strategies and practices those businesses can adopt to build trust, foster emotional connections, and cultivate customer loyalty. The chapter highlights the significance of consistent and reliable service, emotional engagement, loyalty programs, and brand storytelling in building trust. It emphasizes the importance of understanding customer needs, delivering personalized experiences, and leveraging word-of-mouth marketing. By focusing on building trust and fostering loyalty, businesses can create long-lasting relationships with customers and drive sustainable growth.

- Cultivating trust through consistent and reliable service

Cultivating trust through consistent and reliable service is a fundamental aspect of building strong customer relationships. This involves consistently meeting customer expectations, delivering on promises, and providing reliable products or services. By consistently delivering high-quality experiences, businesses can establish a reputation for reliability and dependability, which in turn builds trust with customers.

One way to cultivate trust is by ensuring consistent service delivery across all customer touchpoints. This means providing consistent information, responses, and support through various channels such as in-person interactions, phone calls, emails, and online platforms. Consistency helps create a sense of reliability and reliability breeds trust.

Reliability also extends to product or service quality. Customers expect products or services to perform as advertised and meet their needs consistently. By ensuring consistent quality and addressing any product or service issues promptly, businesses can instill confidence in their customers and build trust over time.

Another important aspect of cultivating trust is setting and managing realistic expectations. Businesses should be transparent and clear about what customers can expect in terms of product features, delivery timelines, pricing, and customer support. Managing expectations effectively helps prevent disappointments and fosters trust by ensuring customers feel informed and aware.

Trust is also built through open and honest communication. Businesses should be proactive in providing updates, addressing customer concerns, and being transparent about any changes or issues that may affect the customer experience. By maintaining open lines of communication, businesses can build trust by demonstrating their commitment to transparency and responsiveness.

Consistency, reliability, transparency, and open communication are all key components of cultivating trust through consistent and reliable service. By focusing on these aspects, businesses can create a trustworthy reputation, which strengthens customer relationships, fosters loyalty, and ultimately drives business success.

•Fostering emotional connections with customers

Fostering emotional connections with customers is a crucial aspect of building strong and lasting relationships. It involves creating a sense of empathy, understanding, and shared values that go beyond transactional interactions. When customers feel emotionally connected to a brand, they develop a deeper level of loyalty and engagement.

One way to foster emotional connections is by understanding and addressing customers' needs, desires, and aspirations. By listening attentively and empathizing with their challenges, businesses can demonstrate that they truly care about their customers' well-being. This could involve tailoring products or services to meet their specific needs or offering personalized recommendations that show an understanding of their preferences.

Storytelling is another powerful tool for fostering emotional connections. By sharing authentic and compelling stories that resonate with customers' emotions, businesses can create a sense of identification and build a deeper connection. These stories can highlight shared values, showcase customer success stories, or illustrate the positive impact of the brand in people's lives.

Another approach is to create meaningful experiences that evoke positive emotions. This could involve surprise gifts, personalized messages, or memorable interactions that go beyond customers' expectations. By consistently delivering exceptional experiences, businesses can evoke positive emotions such as joy, excitement, or gratitude, which in turn deepens the emotional connection.

Building a community or fostering a sense of belonging is also important in fostering emotional connections. By creating platforms or spaces where customers can connect with each other and with the brand, businesses can cultivate a sense of community and belonging. This can be done through social media groups, online forums, or in-person events that encourage customers to share experiences, support each other, and engage with the brand on a deeper level.

Ultimately, fostering emotional connections with customers is about creating experiences that touch their hearts and make them feel valued, understood, and appreciated. By going beyond functional benefits and tapping into their emotions, businesses can forge deep and long-lasting connections that drive customer loyalty, advocacy, and ultimately, business success.

•Implementing loyalty programs and rewards

Implementing loyalty programs and rewards is a powerful strategy for building customer loyalty and fostering long-term relationships. By offering incentives and rewards to customers, businesses can encourage repeat purchases, increase customer engagement, and create a sense of appreciation and value.

One key aspect of implementing loyalty programs is to design them in a way that aligns with customers' preferences and needs. This involves understanding what motivates and incentivizes customers, whether it's exclusive discounts, freebies, points-based systems, or personalized rewards. By tailoring the program to match customers' desires, businesses can increase their appeal and encourage active participation.

Effective communication and promotion of loyalty programs are also essential. Businesses need to clearly communicate the benefits of the program and educate customers on how to earn and redeem rewards. This can be done through various channels, such as email campaigns, social media posts, and in-store signage. By keeping customers informed and engaged, businesses can maximize the impact of their loyalty programs.

Another important aspect is to track and analyze customer data to gain insights into their behavior and preferences. By leveraging data analytics, businesses can identify trends, patterns, and opportunities to enhance the effectiveness of their loyalty programs. This may involve segmenting customers based on their purchasing habits or preferences and offering targeted rewards and incentives.

Implementing a tiered loyalty structure can also be effective in encouraging higher levels of engagement. By offering different tiers or levels of rewards, businesses can create a sense of progression and exclusivity, motivating customers to reach higher tiers and enjoy greater benefits.

Furthermore, businesses can leverage technology to streamline the implementation and management of loyalty programs. This includes using customer relationship management (CRM) software or mobile apps that allow customers to easily track their rewards, redeem offers, and engage with the program. Seamless and user-friendly experiences can enhance customer satisfaction and increase program participation.

Regular evaluation and optimization of loyalty programs are crucial for long-term success. By monitoring program performance, gathering customer feedback, and staying updated on industry trends, businesses can identify areas for improvement and make necessary adjustments to keep the program fresh, relevant, and engaging.

Implementing loyalty programs and rewards is a valuable strategy for cultivating customer loyalty and driving business growth. By designing customer-centric programs, effectively communicating their benefits, leveraging data insights, and embracing technology, businesses can create a compelling loyalty ecosystem that fosters engagement, satisfaction, and long-term customer relationships.

•Harnessing the power of brand storytelling and values

Harnessing the power of brand storytelling and values is a crucial aspect of building strong connections with customers and creating a distinctive brand identity. It involves leveraging narratives, values, and emotions to communicate the essence of a brand and engage customers on a deeper level.

Brand storytelling goes beyond just promoting products or services. It focuses on crafting narratives that resonate with customers, evoke emotions, and create a sense of connection and authenticity. By telling compelling stories, businesses can differentiate themselves in a crowded market, leave a lasting impression, and build a loyal customer base.

To effectively harness brand storytelling, businesses need to define their brand values and core messages. These values should align with the aspirations and beliefs of their target audience. By communicating these values consistently through storytelling, businesses can attract like-minded customers who connect with their brand's purpose and mission.

Authenticity plays a vital role in brand storytelling. Customers are drawn to brands that are genuine and transparent. It is important for businesses to stay true to their values and maintain consistency in their messaging across various touchpoints. By being authentic, businesses can build trust and credibility with customers, fostering long-term relationships.

A strong brand story should also evoke emotions and create a memorable experience for customers. It should tap into their desires, aspirations, and challenges, making them feel understood and valued. By evoking emotions, businesses can leave a lasting impression and forge a deep connection with customers.

Brand storytelling can be delivered through various channels, including websites, social media, advertisements, and content marketing. Visual elements such as videos, images, and graphics can enhance the storytelling experience and make it more impactful. By using compelling visuals, businesses can captivate their audience and reinforce their brand narrative.

Furthermore, businesses can leverage their brand values to align with social causes and make a positive impact. By demonstrating a commitment to social responsibility and sustainability, businesses can attract customers who share the same values. This not only strengthens the brand's reputation but also contributes to building a better society.

Harnessing the power of brand storytelling and values is instrumental in creating a meaningful connection with customers. By crafting authentic and emotionally resonant narratives, businesses can differentiate themselves, build trust, and foster strong customer relationships. By aligning with customers' values and delivering compelling brand experiences, businesses can create a lasting impact and thrive in today's competitive market.

Chapter 7: Customer Success Strategies

This chapter focuses on the importance of customer success in driving business growth. It delves into the strategies and approaches businesses can adopt to ensure the success and satisfaction of their customers. From establishing customer success teams aligned with business goals to adopting proactive and data-driven approaches, this chapter explores how businesses can optimize customer success. It emphasizes the significance of leveraging customer feedback and insights to improve products, services, and processes. By implementing effective customer success strategies, businesses can build strong relationships, enhance customer loyalty, and achieve long-term success.

- Defining customer success and its impact on business growth

Defining customer success is essential in understanding its impact on business growth. Customer success goes beyond the traditional notion of customer satisfaction. It involves ensuring that customers achieve their desired outcomes and attain maximum value from the products or services they have purchased.

The concept of customer success revolves around proactively guiding and supporting customers throughout their journey with a company. It involves understanding their goals, challenges, and expectations and aligning the company's resources and efforts to help them achieve success.

When customers are successful in achieving their desired outcomes, it has a direct impact on business growth. Satisfied and successful customers are more likely to become loyal advocates, referring others to the business and driving new customer acquisition. They are also more likely to renew their contracts or make repeat purchases, leading to increased revenue and profitability.

Moreover, customer success helps build a positive reputation for the business. Satisfied customers are more likely to leave positive reviews, provide testimonials, and share their experiences with others, which can significantly impact brand reputation and attract new customers.

Customer success also plays a crucial role in reducing

customer churn. By understanding and addressing customer needs, resolving issues, and providing ongoing support and guidance, businesses can enhance customer satisfaction and retention. This, in turn, reduces customer churn and the associated costs of acquiring new customers.

Additionally, customer success drives innovation and product improvement. By closely collaborating with customers and gathering their feedback, businesses can gain valuable insights into their needs, preferences, and pain points. This information can be used to enhance existing products, develop new offerings, and stay ahead of the competition.

Defining customer success is vital for businesses to realize its impact on growth. It involves guiding customers to achieve their desired outcomes, fostering loyalty, reducing churn, enhancing brand reputation, and driving innovation. By prioritizing customer success, businesses can cultivate long-term, mutually beneficial relationships with their customers and fuel sustainable growth.

•Establishing customer success teams and aligning them with business goals

Establishing customer success teams and aligning them with business goals is a critical step in ensuring the success and satisfaction of customers. Customer success teams are dedicated groups of professionals who are responsible for proactively managing and nurturing customer relationships. Their primary focus is to understand customer needs, address their challenges, and guide them towards achieving their desired outcomes.

To establish an effective customer success team, businesses must start by defining clear goals and objectives that align with the overall business strategy. These goals may include improving customer satisfaction, increasing customer retention, driving upsells and cross-sells, or promoting advocacy. By aligning the customer success team's objectives with the broader business goals, there is a shared vision and purpose that drives the team's efforts.

Once the goals are established, businesses need to carefully select and assemble the right individuals for the customer success team. This team should consist of individuals who possess strong interpersonal and communication skills, empathy, and a deep understanding of the products or services offered. They should also have a proactive mindset and be capable of building strong relationships with customers.

Training and ongoing development are essential for the success of customer success teams. They need to be equipped with the knowledge and skills required to effectively engage with customers, address their needs, and provide value-added guidance. Training can include product knowledge sessions, communication and negotiation skills development, and customer relationship management techniques.

Another crucial aspect is aligning the customer success team's activities with the customer journey. This involves understanding the different stages of the customer lifecycle and identifying touchpoints where the team can provide support and guidance. By integrating the customer success team's activities seamlessly into the customer journey, businesses can enhance the overall customer experience and drive success.

Regular communication and collaboration with other

departments within the organization are also vital. The customer success team needs to work closely with sales, marketing, product, and support teams to ensure a holistic approach to customer engagement. This collaboration facilitates sharing customer insights, identifying opportunities for improvement, and aligning strategies to deliver exceptional customer experiences.

Finally, businesses should establish metrics and key performance indicators (KPIs) to measure the effectiveness of the customer success team. These metrics can include customer satisfaction scores, retention rates, upsell/cross-sell rates, and customer advocacy metrics. By regularly monitoring and analyzing these metrics, businesses can identify areas for improvement and continuously enhance the performance of the customer success team.

Establishing customer success teams and aligning them with business goals is crucial for driving customer satisfaction and success. By defining clear objectives, assembling the right team, providing proper training, integrating with the customer journey, fostering collaboration, and measuring performance, businesses can effectively manage customer relationships and contribute to long-term business growth.

•Adopting proactive and data-driven approaches to drive customer success

Adopting proactive and data-driven approaches is essential for driving customer success. It involves using data and insights to anticipate customer needs, identify potential issues, and take proactive measures to ensure customer satisfaction and achieve their desired outcomes.

One aspect of adopting proactive approaches is leveraging customer data to gain a deep understanding of their behavior, preferences, and pain points. By analyzing customer data, businesses can identify patterns, trends, and opportunities to proactively address customer needs. This can involve using analytics tools to track customer interactions, collecting feedback through surveys and monitoring social media channels, and analyzing customer support tickets and inquiries.

Using data-driven approaches also means utilizing predictive analytics to forecast customer behavior and identify potential risks or opportunities. By applying predictive modeling techniques, businesses can anticipate customer churn, identify upsell or cross-sell opportunities, and personalize customer experiences based on their unique preferences and behaviors.

To drive customer success, businesses should establish proactive communication channels with their customers. This includes sending proactive notifications, updates, and reminders to keep customers informed and engaged. For example, sending personalized emails to provide product recommendations or relevant resources based on their previous interactions.

Furthermore, businesses can leverage automation and artificial intelligence (AI) technologies to scale proactive customer success efforts. By automating certain processes and using AI-powered chatbots, businesses can deliver timely and relevant information to customers, provide instant support, and offer personalized recommendations.

Another key aspect of proactive approaches is continuously monitoring customer health and engagement metrics. By tracking metrics such as product usage, adoption rates, and customer satisfaction scores, businesses can identify early warning signs and intervene proactively to address any potential issues. This can involve reaching out to customers who show signs of disengagement or providing additional resources and support to ensure their success.

In addition to being proactive, it is crucial to measure and track the impact of these approaches on customer success. Businesses should define key performance indicators (KPIs) that align with their customer success goals and regularly analyze the data to assess the effectiveness of their strategies. This allows businesses to make data-driven decisions and continuously optimize their proactive approaches for driving customer success.

Adopting proactive and data-driven approaches is vital for driving customer success. By leveraging customer data, applying predictive analytics, establishing proactive communication channels, automating processes, and continuously monitoring customer health metrics, businesses can anticipate customer needs, address potential issues, and foster long-term customer success. This approach helps businesses build strong customer relationships, enhance customer satisfaction, and drive sustainable growth.

•Leveraging customer feedback to improve products, services, and processes

Leveraging customer feedback is a crucial aspect of improving products, services, and processes. It involves actively seeking and collecting feedback from customers to gain valuable insights into their experiences, preferences, and pain points. By analyzing and utilizing this feedback, businesses can make informed decisions and implement necessary improvements to enhance customer satisfaction and drive business growth.

To leverage customer feedback effectively, businesses should establish feedback mechanisms that make it easy for customers to provide their opinions and suggestions. This can include online surveys, feedback forms, customer reviews, and social media monitoring. By offering multiple channels for feedback, businesses can capture a diverse range of perspectives and gather a comprehensive understanding of customer sentiment.

Once feedback is collected, it is essential to analyze and interpret it to identify trends, patterns, and areas for improvement. This analysis can involve categorizing feedback based on common themes, quantifying feedback using metrics, and prioritizing areas that require immediate attention. By applying data analysis techniques, businesses can extract actionable insights from customer feedback and make informed decisions about product enhancements, service improvements, and process optimizations.

Leveraging customer feedback also involves closing the feedback loop by acknowledging customer input and communicating the actions taken based on their feedback. This demonstrates that the business values customer opinions and is committed to continuously improving based on their needs. It helps build trust and strengthens the customer-business relationship.

In addition to making improvements based on customer feedback, businesses can use customer insights to identify opportunities for innovation and develop new products or services that align with customer needs. By understanding customer pain points and unmet needs, businesses can stay ahead of the competition and deliver innovative solutions that differentiate them in the market.

Furthermore, businesses can leverage customer feedback to refine their customer service processes and provide more personalized and tailored support. By analyzing customer feedback related to customer service interactions, businesses can identify areas where improvements can be made, such as response times, issue resolution, and communication channels. This allows businesses to provide a better customer experience and foster stronger relationships with their customers.

Leveraging customer feedback is essential for continuous improvement and business growth. By actively seeking and analyzing customer feedback, businesses can gain valuable insights, make informed decisions, and implement necessary changes to enhance their products, services, and processes. This customer-centric approach helps businesses meet customer expectations, improve customer satisfaction, and ultimately drive long-term success.

Chapter 8: Building Customer Advocacy

This chapter focuses on the importance of turning customers into brand advocates and ambassadors. It explores strategies and techniques to foster strong customer relationships, loyalty, and advocacy. The chapter delves into implementing referral programs, cultivating a community of loyal customers, and harnessing the power of word-of-mouth marketing. By building a base of enthusiastic brand advocates, businesses can benefit from increased customer acquisition, positive brand reputation, and enhanced credibility. The chapter provides insights and practical tips to empower businesses in creating a network of passionate customers who willingly promote and endorse their products or services.

•Turning customers into brand advocates and ambassadors

urning customers into brand advocates and ambassadors is a crucial aspect of building a strong and influential customer base. This process involves transforming satisfied customers into loyal advocates who actively promote and endorse a brand. By leveraging the power of word-of-mouth marketing, businesses can benefit from the genuine enthusiasm and positive recommendations of their customers.

To turn customers into brand advocates, it is essential to provide exceptional experiences and exceed their expectations consistently. When customers have a positive experience with a brand, they are more likely to share their satisfaction with others. This can be achieved by delivering high-quality products or services, offering personalized interactions, and resolving any issues promptly and effectively.

Building a strong emotional connection with customers is another key element in creating brand advocates. When customers feel emotionally invested in a brand, they are more inclined to recommend it to others. This can be accomplished by fostering authentic relationships, demonstrating empathy, and showcasing shared values.

Implementing referral programs is an effective strategy to encourage customers to become brand advocates. By offering incentives or rewards for referrals, businesses can tap into the existing customer network and expand their reach through word-of-mouth recommendations.

Cultivating a community of loyal customers can also contribute to turning customers into brand advocates. By providing exclusive benefits, engaging them in special events or activities, and creating a sense of belonging, businesses can foster a dedicated and passionate community that naturally advocates for the brand.

Engaging customers through social media and online platforms is another avenue to turn them into brand ambassadors. By encouraging user-generated content, running contests or challenges, and sharing customer success stories, businesses can amplify their brand message and leverage the influence of their customers' networks.

Overall, turning customers into brand advocates requires delivering exceptional experiences, building emotional connections, implementing referral programs, cultivating communities, and leveraging social media. By prioritizing these strategies, businesses can transform satisfied customers into powerful brand ambassadors who willingly promote and endorse their products or services, leading to increased visibility, credibility, and customer acquisition.

•Implementing referral programs to drive new customer acquisition

Implementing referral programs is an effective strategy employed by businesses to drive new customer acquisition through the power of word-of-mouth marketing. Referral programs leverage the existing customer base to generate new leads and expand the customer network.

Referral programs work by incentivizing current customers to recommend the brand or its products/services to their friends, family, or colleagues. This can be achieved through various mechanisms such as offering discounts, rewards, or exclusive benefits to both the referrer and the referred customer.

One of the key advantages of referral programs is the trust factor. Customers tend to trust recommendations from their peers more than traditional marketing messages. When a satisfied customer personally vouches for a brand, it creates a level of credibility and increases the likelihood of acquiring new customers.

To implement an effective referral program, businesses

need to design clear and attractive incentives that motivate customers to participate. The incentives should provide value to both the referrer and the referred customer, encouraging them to engage in the program. This can be in the form of discounts on future purchases, freebies, cash rewards, or even exclusive access to premium features.

To maximize the success of referral programs, businesses should make the process simple and seamless. Providing customers with user-friendly referral tools, such as personalized referral links or easy-to-share social media buttons, enhances the likelihood of them actually referring others. Additionally, offering clear instructions and guidance on how to participate in the referral program ensures that customers understand the process and feel confident in making referrals.

Measuring and tracking the results of referral programs is essential to assess their effectiveness. By monitoring the number of referrals, conversion rates, and the overall impact on customer acquisition, businesses can optimize their referral strategies and make necessary adjustments to maximize their success.

Implementing referral programs can be a cost-effective and powerful way for businesses to acquire new customers. By harnessing the power of customer advocacy and incentivizing referrals, businesses can tap into the existing customer network and expand their reach, leading to increased brand visibility, trust, and ultimately, customer acquisition.

•Cultivating a strong community of loyal customers

Cultivating a strong community of loyal customers is a crucial aspect of building a successful and sustainable business. A loyal customer community consists of individuals who not only make repeat purchases but also actively engage with the brand, advocate for it, and contribute to its growth.

To cultivate a strong customer community, businesses need to prioritize relationship-building and create a sense of belonging among their customers. This can be achieved through various strategies and initiatives:

1. **Engaging Communication:** Regular and meaningful communication with customers is

key to building a strong community. Businesses can leverage email newsletters, social media platforms, and other communication channels to share relevant content, provide updates, and foster dialogue with customers.

2. **Exclusive Benefits:** Offering exclusive benefits to community members helps strengthen their loyalty. This can include access to special promotions, early product launches, personalized discounts, or loyalty rewards that are specifically tailored for community members.

3. **User-Generated Content:** Encouraging customers to share their experiences and opinions through user-generated content builds a sense of community. This can be in the form of testimonials, reviews, social media posts, or blog contributions. Businesses can showcase and amplify this content to demonstrate the active engagement and satisfaction of their customer community.

4. **Community Events:** Hosting virtual or in-person events exclusively for community members

fosters a sense of connection and belonging. These events can include webinars, workshops, networking sessions, or even customer appreciation events. By bringing customers together, businesses provide opportunities for networking, learning, and sharing experiences.

5. **Customer Support and Feedback:** Prioritizing exceptional customer support and actively seeking customer feedback demonstrates a commitment to customer satisfaction. Businesses should provide multiple channels for customers to reach out, address concerns promptly, and actively listen to their feedback. This not only resolves issues but also reinforces the sense of community by showing that customers' voices are valued.

6. **Advocacy Programs:** Encouraging customers to become advocates for the brand strengthens the customer community. Businesses can implement referral programs, ambassador programs, or loyalty programs that incentivize customers to spread the word about the brand and actively promote it within their networks.

By implementing these strategies, businesses can create a sense of community that goes beyond transactional relationships. A strong customer community fosters loyalty, word-of-mouth marketing, and long-term business growth. It becomes a valuable asset that supports the brand's success and sustainability in the marketplace.

•Leveraging the power of word-of-mouth marketing

Leveraging the power of word-of-mouth marketing is a strategic approach that businesses can employ to drive brand awareness, credibility, and customer acquisition. Word-of-mouth marketing occurs when satisfied customers voluntarily share positive experiences and recommendations about a brand with others. It is a powerful and influential form of marketing as people tend to trust recommendations from friends, family, or peers more than traditional advertising.

To effectively leverage word-of-mouth marketing, businesses can implement the following strategies:

Delightful Customer Experiences: Providing exceptional

products, services, and customer experiences is the foundation of generating positive word-of-mouth. When customers have a memorable and satisfying experience with a brand, they are more likely to share their positive experiences with others.

Encouraging and Rewarding Referrals: Actively encouraging customers to refer their friends and family to the brand can amplify word-of-mouth marketing. Implementing referral programs that offer incentives or rewards for successful referrals motivates customers to spread the word and increases the likelihood of new customer acquisition through referrals.

Influencer Marketing: Collaborating with influencers or brand advocates who have a significant following and influence in the target market can amplify word-of-mouth marketing efforts. Influencers can authentically promote the brand to their audience, generating trust and interest in the products or services.

Online Reviews and Testimonials: Actively seeking and showcasing online reviews and testimonials from satisfied customers can significantly impact potential customers' perception of the brand. Positive reviews and testimonials serve as social proof, building trust and credibility and encouraging others to try the brand.

Engaging on social media: Active engagement on social media platforms allows businesses to connect with their audience, respond to queries and comments, and foster conversations around their brand. By engaging with customers in a timely and authentic manner, businesses can encourage positive word-of-mouth and build a strong online reputation.

User-Generated Content: Encouraging customers to create and share user-generated content related to the brand can amplify word-of-mouth marketing. This can include sharing photos, videos, or stories about their experiences with the brand, which can inspire others to engage and consider the brand.

Exceptional Customer Service: Providing outstanding customer service experiences creates positive impressions and generates word-of-mouth recommendations. Promptly addressing customer concerns, going the extra mile to exceed expectations, and ensuring customer satisfaction contribute to positive word-of-mouth.

By leveraging the power of word-of-mouth marketing, businesses can tap into the influence of satisfied customers to expand their reach, build trust, and attract new customers. It is a cost-effective and impactful marketing strategy that can have long-lasting effects on brand reputation and business growth.

Chapter 9: Customer Feedback and Continuous Improvement

This chapter focuses on the critical role of customer feedback in driving continuous improvement within an organization. It explores various methods and techniques to gather valuable insights from customers, such as surveys, feedback loops, and sentiment analysis. The chapter emphasizes the importance of analyzing and interpreting customer feedback to identify areas of improvement. It also highlights the significance of incorporating customer insights into product development, service enhancements, and overall business strategies. By prioritizing customer feedback and implementing a culture of continuous improvement, businesses can strengthen customer satisfaction, loyalty, and overall organizational success.

- Gathering and analyzing customer feedback through surveys and feedback loops

Gathering and analyzing customer feedback through surveys and feedback loops is a crucial aspect of understanding customer preferences and improving business processes. Surveys provide an opportunity to directly engage with customers and gather their opinions, satisfaction levels, and suggestions. By designing well-crafted surveys, businesses can gather specific insights about various aspects of their products, services, and customer experiences.

Feedback loops, on the other hand, involve actively seeking feedback from customers after specific interactions or touchpoints. This can be done through follow-up emails, post-purchase surveys, or customer service interactions. Feedback loops provide real-time insights and allow businesses to address any issues or concerns promptly.

Once the feedback is collected, the next step is to analyze it effectively. This involves sorting and categorizing the feedback based on various parameters such as satisfaction levels, common themes, and specific areas for improvement. Analyzing customer feedback helps identify patterns, trends, and areas where the business excels or needs improvement.

By analyzing customer feedback, businesses can gain valuable insights into customer preferences, pain points, and expectations. This information can guide decision-making processes, product/service enhancements, and customer-centric strategies. It allows businesses to identify areas of improvement and prioritize actions that will have the most significant impact on customer satisfaction and loyalty.

Gathering and analyzing customer feedback demonstrates to customers that their opinions are valued and that the business is committed to continuously improving its offerings. This fosters trust, strengthens the customer-business relationship, and encourages customers to provide ongoing feedback in the future.

The systematic gathering and analysis of customer feedback through surveys and feedback loops help businesses make informed decisions, enhance customer experiences, and drive continuous improvement. By leveraging these valuable insights, businesses can stay responsive to customer needs, build stronger relationships, and ultimately achieve long-term success.

•Implementing strategies to address customer pain points and enhance satisfaction

Implementing strategies to address customer pain points and enhance satisfaction is a fundamental aspect of effective customer relationship management. By identifying and addressing the challenges and concerns that customers face, businesses can improve their overall satisfaction levels and build long-term loyalty.

To start, businesses need to have a deep understanding of their customers' pain points. This involves actively listening to customer feedback, conducting surveys, and analyzing customer interactions to identify recurring issues or areas of dissatisfaction. Once pain points are identified, businesses can develop targeted strategies to address them.

One strategy is to enhance product or service features based on customer feedback. By incorporating customer suggestions and addressing common pain points, businesses can provide a better product experience and meet the specific needs of their target audience.

Another strategy is to improve customer support and service. This can include implementing faster response times, increasing accessibility through multiple channels, and training support staff to handle customer inquiries and issues effectively. By providing prompt and reliable support, businesses can alleviate customer frustrations and enhance satisfaction.

Furthermore, businesses can focus on streamlining processes to eliminate potential pain points. This involves analyzing customer journeys and identifying bottlenecks or areas where customers may experience challenges. By optimizing these processes, businesses can reduce customer effort, improve efficiency, and deliver a more seamless experience.

Personalization is also an effective strategy for addressing customer pain points. By tailoring products, services, and communications to individual customer preferences and needs, businesses can create a more engaging and relevant experience. This can be achieved through data analysis, segmentation, and targeted marketing campaigns.

Continuous monitoring and improvement are essential in implementing these strategies. Regularly collecting customer feedback, measuring satisfaction metrics, and tracking performance allows businesses to identify emerging pain points and make necessary adjustments in real-time.

Implementing strategies to address customer pain points and enhance satisfaction requires a customer-centric approach. By actively listening to customers, proactively addressing their concerns, and continuously improving products and processes, businesses can create a positive customer experience that fosters loyalty and drives long-term success.

•Leveraging customer insights for product development and innovation

Leveraging customer insights for product development and innovation is a crucial aspect of staying competitive in today's dynamic business landscape. By actively seeking and utilizing feedback from customers, businesses can gain valuable insights that drive meaningful improvements and foster innovation.

One way to leverage customer insights is through conducting surveys, focus groups, or interviews to understand customers' needs, preferences, and pain points. By directly engaging with customers, businesses can uncover valuable information about their expectations, challenges, and desires. This information can then be used to inform product development and innovation strategies.

Customer feedback can also play a significant role in identifying opportunities for improvement and innovation. By analyzing feedback, businesses can identify patterns and trends that highlight areas where their products or services may be falling short or where new solutions can be introduced. This customer-driven approach to product development ensures that businesses are addressing real market needs and delivering solutions that resonate with their target audience.

In addition to direct customer feedback, businesses can leverage data analytics and market research to gain deeper insights into customer behavior and preferences. Through techniques such as data mining and segmentation, businesses can identify customer segments with specific needs and tailor their product development efforts accordingly. This data-driven approach allows for more targeted and effective innovation.

Collaboration with customers is another way to leverage their insights for product development and innovation. This can involve involving customers in beta testing, co-creation, or ideation sessions. By involving customers in the development process, businesses gain firsthand feedback, ideas, and perspectives that can lead to more innovative and customer-centric solutions.

Ultimately, leveraging customer insights for product development and innovation enables businesses to create products and services that align closely with customer needs and preferences. It helps businesses stay ahead of the competition by delivering value-added solutions and continuously improving their offerings based on customer feedback. By actively involving customers in the development process and utilizing data-driven approaches, businesses can drive innovation, enhance customer satisfaction, and achieve long-term success.

•Incorporating continuous improvement into organizational culture

Incorporating continuous improvement into organizational culture is a strategic approach that fosters a mindset of constant growth, learning, and refinement within an organization. It involves creating an environment where employees are encouraged and empowered to identify areas for improvement, propose innovative solutions, and implement changes that lead to enhanced performance and outcomes.

One key aspect of incorporating continuous improvement into organizational culture is establishing a culture of learning and openness to change. This includes promoting a growth mindset, where employees are encouraged to view challenges as opportunities for growth and development. It also involves providing opportunities for ongoing training, skill development, and knowledge sharing to empower employees with the tools and resources they need to drive improvement.

Another important element is the establishment of feedback mechanisms and channels for communication. This allows employees to share their ideas, concerns, and suggestions for improvement. Whether through regular meetings, suggestion boxes, or digital platforms, creating avenues for open and transparent communication enables employees at all levels to contribute to the continuous improvement process.

Incorporating continuous improvement into organizational culture also involves setting clear goals and performance metrics. This provides a benchmark for measuring progress and identifying areas where improvement is needed. By aligning individual and team goals with the broader organizational objectives, employees can see the direct impact of their efforts and understand how their contributions contribute to the overall success of the organization.

Furthermore, organizations need to foster a supportive and collaborative environment that encourages experimentation and risk-taking. This involves recognizing and celebrating both successes and failures as learning opportunities. Encouraging employees to take calculated risks and learn from their experiences fosters innovation, creativity, and a culture of continuous improvement.

Leadership plays a crucial role in driving and sustaining a culture of continuous improvement. Leaders need to lead by example, demonstrating their commitment to ongoing learning, improvement, and innovation. They should provide resources, support, and guidance to employees, enabling them to drive improvement initiatives and fostering a sense of ownership and accountability.

Incorporating continuous improvement into organizational culture requires creating an environment that values learning, embraces change, and encourages collaboration. By empowering employees, establishing feedback mechanisms, setting clear goals, and fostering a supportive culture, organizations can drive innovation, enhance performance, and adapt to evolving market dynamics. It is a journey that requires commitment and effort but can lead to long-term success and competitive advantage.

Chapter 10: Customer Retention and Churn Management

This chapter deals with the critical aspect of retaining valuable customers and effectively managing customer churn. It explores strategies and tactics to increase customer loyalty, reduce churn rates, and foster long-term relationships. The chapter delves into techniques such as customer segmentation, personalized retention campaigns, loyalty programs, and proactive churn prediction. By implementing these approaches, businesses can optimize their customer retention efforts, enhance customer satisfaction, and minimize revenue loss due to customer attrition. Ultimately, this chapter equips organizations with the knowledge and tools needed to retain and nurture their customer base for sustainable growth and success.

- Understanding the factors influencing customer churn

Understanding the factors influencing customer churn is crucial for businesses to proactively address and mitigate customer attrition. Several key factors can contribute to customer churn, and by identifying and understanding them, organizations can take appropriate actions to retain their customers.

One important factor is poor customer satisfaction. Dissatisfied customers are more likely to churn as they may seek alternatives that better meet their needs or expectations. By monitoring customer satisfaction levels through surveys, feedback, and customer interactions, businesses can identify areas of improvement and take corrective measures to enhance satisfaction.

Another factor is inadequate customer support or service. When customers experience issues or problems and find it difficult to receive timely and effective support, they may become frustrated and choose to discontinue their relationship with the business. Organizations should focus on providing exceptional customer service, quick issue resolution, and accessible support channels to prevent churn.

Competitive offerings and pricing can also influence customer churn. If customers find better alternatives in terms of product features, pricing, or value for money, they may switch to competitors. It is essential for businesses to regularly analyze the competitive landscape, monitor market trends, and ensure their offerings remain competitive and compelling.

Lack of engagement and personalized experiences can also contribute to churn. Customers expect personalized interactions and relevant experiences tailored to their needs and preferences. By leveraging customer data and implementing personalized marketing and communication strategies, businesses can increase engagement and build stronger connections with their customers, reducing the likelihood of churn.

Lastly, changes in customer circumstances or needs can lead to churn. This may include changes in business requirements, financial constraints, or organizational restructuring. By actively engaging with customers, understanding their evolving needs, and providing flexible solutions, businesses can adapt and retain customers even during challenging times.

Understanding these factors and their impact on customer churn allows businesses to develop targeted strategies to reduce churn rates. By addressing customer satisfaction, improving customer support, staying competitive, personalizing experiences, and adapting to changing needs, organizations can enhance customer retention, foster loyalty, and drive long-term business success.

•Implementing effective customer retention strategies

Implementing effective customer retention strategies is crucial for businesses to cultivate long-term relationships with their customers, drive loyalty, and maximize their lifetime value. These strategies focus on engaging, satisfying, and delighting existing customers to minimize churn and encourage repeat purchases.

One key aspect of effective customer retention is delivering exceptional customer experiences. By consistently exceeding customer expectations at every touchpoint, businesses can create positive emotional connections and foster customer loyalty. This involves personalized interactions, proactive communication, and resolving issues promptly and satisfactorily.

Customer loyalty programs are another powerful retention strategy. These programs reward customers for their continued support and incentivize repeat purchases. By offering exclusive discounts, rewards, or special privileges, businesses can motivate customers to stay loyal and feel valued.

Regular and targeted communication is also vital for customer retention. By staying in touch with customers through personalized emails, newsletters, or relevant content, businesses can nurture relationships, provide valuable information, and remind customers of their value. This helps maintain top-of-mind awareness and strengthens the bond between the customer and the brand.

Building strong relationships with customers is essential. This involves actively listening to their feedback, understanding their needs, and going the extra mile to meet their expectations. By fostering open and transparent communication, businesses can address concerns, offer solutions, and demonstrate their commitment to customer satisfaction.

Continuous improvement is a fundamental aspect of customer retention. By constantly evaluating and enhancing products, services, and processes based on customer feedback and market trends, businesses can stay ahead of the competition and ensure their offerings remain relevant and compelling.

Furthermore, providing excellent post-purchase support and customer service is crucial for retention. Promptly resolving any issues, offering technical assistance, and providing ongoing support demonstrate a commitment to customer success and satisfaction.

Lastly, creating a culture of customer-centricity throughout the organization is essential. By instilling a customer-focused mindset and empowering employees to prioritize customer needs, businesses can create a seamless and enjoyable customer experience at every touchpoint.

By implementing these customer retention strategies, businesses can significantly reduce churn rates, increase customer loyalty, and drive sustainable growth. Retaining existing customers is not only more cost-effective than acquiring new ones but also leads to higher customer lifetime value and positive word-of-mouth referrals, further fueling business success.

•Monitoring and predicting customer behavior to prevent churn

Monitoring and predicting customer behavior is a crucial aspect of customer retention and churn prevention. By closely monitoring customer interactions, preferences, and engagement patterns, businesses can gain valuable insights into their behavior and take proactive measures to prevent churn.

One effective way to monitor customer behavior is through data analysis. By leveraging customer data, businesses can identify key indicators and patterns that signal a customer's likelihood to churn. This data can include metrics such as purchase frequency, engagement with marketing campaigns, customer service interactions, and feedback sentiment analysis. By analyzing these data points, businesses can detect early warning signs and take timely action.

Predictive analytics plays a significant role in forecasting customer behavior. By utilizing advanced algorithms and models, businesses can predict the probability of customer churn based on historical data and patterns. This enables proactive intervention and personalized retention strategies for customers who are at risk of churning. By identifying specific triggers or factors that contribute to churn, businesses can tailor their approach and address those factors effectively.

One effective strategy for preventing churn is implementing proactive customer outreach. By reaching out to customers who exhibit signs of disengagement or reduced activity, businesses can understand their concerns, address issues, and offer solutions. This can be done through personalized communication, such as targeted emails, phone calls, or personalized offers, to re-engage customers and show them that their business is valued.

Another approach is to leverage customer segmentation and create tailored retention campaigns. By segmenting customers based on behavior, preferences, or demographics, businesses can develop targeted campaigns that address specific needs and pain points. This allows for more personalized and relevant interactions, increasing the chances of customer satisfaction and loyalty.

Monitoring customer feedback and satisfaction is also essential for churn prevention. By regularly collecting customer feedback through surveys, reviews, or social media monitoring, businesses can gain insights into customer sentiment and identify areas for improvement. Addressing customer concerns promptly and effectively not only improves customer satisfaction but also reduces the likelihood of churn.

Monitoring and predicting customer behavior is a vital practice for preventing churn. By analyzing customer data, leveraging predictive analytics, implementing proactive outreach, and tailoring retention strategies, businesses can proactively address customer concerns, improve engagement, and foster long-term loyalty. By understanding customer behavior and taking proactive measures, businesses can minimize churn rates and build strong, lasting customer relationships.

•Designing loyalty programs and initiatives for retention

Designing effective loyalty programs and initiatives is crucial for customer retention. These programs aim to reward and incentivize customers for their continued loyalty, encouraging them to stay engaged and make repeat purchases. By offering unique benefits and experiences, businesses can create a sense of value and exclusivity, fostering long-term customer relationships.

One key aspect of designing a successful loyalty program is identifying the right rewards and incentives. This involves understanding the preferences and motivations of the target customer base. Rewards can include discounts, exclusive offers, freebies, access to

VIP events, personalized recommendations, or even a tiered system that unlocks more benefits as customers move up the loyalty ladder. By offering desirable rewards, businesses can keep customers engaged and motivated to continue their relationship.

Creating a seamless and user-friendly experience is essential for loyalty program success. Businesses should design a program that is easy to understand, join, and participate in. This includes providing clear instructions on how to earn and redeem rewards, as well as ensuring that the redemption process is convenient and hassle-free. Utilizing technology, such as mobile apps or online platforms, can enhance the user experience and make it easier for customers to engage with the loyalty program.

Personalization is another key factor in designing effective loyalty programs. Tailoring rewards and offers to individual customer preferences and behavior can significantly enhance their experience. By leveraging customer data and insights, businesses can provide personalized recommendations, offers, and rewards that align with each customer's specific needs and interests. This personal touch not only increases the perceived value of the program but also strengthens the emotional connection between the customer and the brand.

Communication and engagement are vital in loyalty program design. Regularly updating customers about new rewards, promotions, or exclusive events can keep them excited and engaged. Utilizing various communication channels, such as email newsletters, push notifications, or social media updates, helps businesses stay connected with their loyal customers and maintain top-of-mind awareness.

Continuous evaluation and improvement are essential for the long-term success of loyalty programs. By monitoring program performance, tracking customer engagement, and gathering feedback, businesses can identify areas for enhancement and make necessary adjustments. This includes analyzing redemption rates, customer satisfaction scores, and overall program effectiveness. Making data-driven decisions and iterating on the program based on customer feedback can lead to better outcomes and increased customer loyalty.

Designing effective loyalty programs and initiatives is crucial for customer retention. By offering desirable rewards, creating a seamless experience, personalizing offerings, maintaining open communication, and continuously evaluating and improving the program, businesses can foster long-term customer loyalty and maximize customer retention rates. A well-designed loyalty program can not only increase customer engagement but also drive revenue growth and enhance brand reputation.

Chapter 11: Personalization and Customization

This chapter explores the importance of tailoring experiences to individual customer needs and preferences. By leveraging data and insights, businesses can create personalized marketing campaigns, customize products and services, and deliver targeted recommendations. This chapter delves into the benefits of personalization in enhancing customer satisfaction, engagement, and loyalty. It discusses strategies for collecting and analyzing customer data, implementing personalized marketing techniques, and striking the right balance between personalization and privacy. With practical examples and best practices, this chapter equips businesses with the knowledge and tools to create personalized experiences that resonate with their customers and drive long-term success.

- Leveraging data to deliver personalized experiences

In today's data-driven world, leveraging customer data is essential for delivering personalized experiences. This involves collecting, analyzing, and interpreting data to gain insights into customer preferences, behaviors, and needs. By understanding individual customer profiles, businesses can tailor their interactions and offerings accordingly. They can segment their customer base and create targeted marketing campaigns that resonate with specific customer groups. Personalization can extend to product recommendations, content delivery, and communication channels, providing a seamless and customized experience.

Data can be gathered from various sources, including customer interactions, purchase history, website behavior, social media engagement, and more. Advanced analytics tools and techniques help businesses make sense of this data, uncover patterns, and identify valuable insights. By analyzing customer data, businesses can identify trends, preferences, and pain points, enabling them to make informed decisions about product development, marketing strategies, and customer service enhancements.

Implementing personalization requires a robust data management system and infrastructure that ensures data security, privacy, and compliance with relevant regulations. It also requires a customer-centric mindset and culture that values and prioritizes the customer experience.

When data is leveraged effectively, businesses can create personalized experiences that make customers feel valued and understood. From personalized recommendations and targeted offers to customized communication and tailored user interfaces, businesses can deliver relevant and meaningful interactions that resonate with individual customers. This enhances customer satisfaction, engagement, and loyalty, ultimately driving business growth and profitability.

However, it's important to strike a balance between personalization and privacy. Respecting customer privacy and obtaining explicit consent for data usage are crucial considerations. Transparency and clear communication regarding data collection and usage practices help build trust and ensure customers feel comfortable sharing their information.

Leveraging customer data to deliver personalized experiences is a powerful strategy for enhancing customer satisfaction and building long-term relationships. By understanding individual preferences and tailoring interactions accordingly, businesses can create meaningful connections and drive business success.

•Implementing personalized marketing campaigns and recommendations

Implementing personalized marketing campaigns and recommendations is a strategic approach that leverages customer data and insights to deliver targeted and relevant messaging to individual customers. By tailoring marketing efforts to meet the specific needs and preferences of customers, businesses can enhance engagement, drive conversions, and build long-lasting relationships.

To implement personalized marketing campaigns, businesses need to gather and analyze customer data from various sources such as purchase history, browsing behavior, demographics, and preferences. This data provides valuable insights into customer preferences, enabling businesses to create tailored messages that resonate with their audience. By understanding customer needs, businesses can craft compelling marketing content that speaks directly to individual interests and pain points.

Recommendation engines play a crucial role in delivering personalized recommendations to customers. These engines utilize algorithms and machine learning techniques to analyze customer data and provide product suggestions based on their browsing history, purchase behavior, and preferences. By offering personalized product recommendations, businesses can enhance the customer experience, increase cross-selling and upselling opportunities, and drive customer loyalty.

Personalized marketing campaigns can be executed through various channels such as email marketing, social media advertising, website personalization, and targeted content marketing. By delivering the right message to the right customer at the right time, businesses can maximize the impact of their marketing efforts and increase customer engagement.

Implementing personalized marketing campaigns requires robust marketing automation tools and technologies that can segment customer data, create dynamic content, and automate campaign delivery. These tools enable businesses to streamline their marketing processes, optimize campaign performance, and track customer responses.

It's important for businesses to strike a balance between personalization and privacy. Respecting customer privacy and ensuring data security are essential considerations. Obtaining explicit consent for data usage and providing transparency regarding data collection and usage practices help build trust with customers.

Implementing personalized marketing campaigns and recommendations allows businesses to deliver targeted and relevant messages to individual customers. By leveraging customer data and insights, businesses can enhance customer engagement, drive conversions, and build strong customer relationships. Personalized marketing enables businesses to stand out in a crowded marketplace, meet customer expectations, and create memorable brand experiences.

•Customizing products and services based on individual customer needs

Customizing products and services based on individual customer needs is a powerful approach that allows businesses to deliver tailored solutions that meet specific customer requirements. By understanding the unique preferences, challenges, and goals of each customer, businesses can provide personalized experiences that drive satisfaction, loyalty, and long-term success.

To customize products and services, businesses need to gather comprehensive customer data and insights. This can include information such as demographic data, purchase history, browsing behavior, feedback, and customer preferences. By analyzing this data, businesses can identify patterns and trends that inform the customization process.

Customization involves adapting products and services to align with individual customer preferences. This can include offering different product variations, personalized packaging, flexible pricing options, or specialized features that cater to specific needs. By offering tailored solutions, businesses can address the unique requirements of each customer, providing them with a superior experience and enhancing their satisfaction.

The customization process requires robust technology and systems to support flexible manufacturing, supply chain management, and customer data analysis. With the help of advanced technology, businesses can streamline the customization process, ensuring efficient production and delivery while maintaining high-quality standards.

Furthermore, effective communication and collaboration with customers play a vital role in the customization process. By actively engaging with customers and seeking their input, businesses can gain valuable insights into their preferences, needs, and expectations. This feedback can be used to refine and improve the customization offerings, ensuring that they truly align with customer requirements.

Customizing products and services goes beyond meeting immediate customer needs; it also fosters customer loyalty and advocacy. When customers feel that a business understands and caters to their individual needs, they are more likely to develop a sense of loyalty and trust. Satisfied customers are more inclined to become brand advocates, spreading positive word-of-mouth and recommending the business to others.

Customizing products and services based on individual customer needs is a powerful strategy to enhance customer satisfaction, loyalty, and business success. By leveraging customer data, implementing robust technology, and actively engaging with customers, businesses can create tailored solutions that address specific customer requirements. Through customization, businesses can differentiate themselves in the market, build stronger customer relationships, and drive long-term growth.

•Balancing personalization with privacy and data protection

In today's digital age, where personalization has become a key strategy in enhancing customer experiences, businesses must also prioritize privacy and data protection. Balancing personalization with privacy is crucial to build and maintain trust with customers, ensuring their data is handled responsibly and ethically.

To strike this balance, businesses need to establish robust data protection measures and adhere to relevant privacy regulations. This includes implementing secure data storage, encryption techniques, access controls, and regular audits to safeguard customer information. By demonstrating a commitment to data protection, businesses can assure customers that their personal data is being handled with the utmost care.

Transparency is another important aspect of balancing personalization and privacy. Businesses should clearly communicate their data collection and usage practices, providing customers with information on how their data is being utilized to personalize their experiences. This transparency helps customers make informed decisions about sharing their data and builds trust in the business.

Consent plays a central role in maintaining privacy while personalizing experiences. Businesses should obtain explicit consent from customers before collecting and using their personal information. This ensures that customers have control over their data and can choose the level of personalization they are comfortable with. Providing easy opt-out options and allowing customers to update their preferences further empowers them in managing their privacy.

Anonymization and aggregation techniques can also be employed to balance personalization and privacy. By de-identifying personal data and grouping it with similar data sets, businesses can derive valuable insights for personalization without compromising individual privacy. This approach helps protect customer identities while still enabling effective personalization strategies.

Regular audits and assessments of data practices are essential to ensure ongoing compliance with privacy regulations and industry best practices. Businesses should review their data handling processes, security measures, and consent management systems to identify and address any potential privacy risks.

Balancing personalization with privacy and data protection is crucial in today's digital landscape. By implementing strong data protection measures, being transparent about data practices, obtaining consent, and employing anonymization techniques, businesses can provide personalized experiences while respecting customer privacy. Striking this balance builds trust, enhances customer relationships, and strengthens the overall reputation of the business.

Chapter 12: Measuring Customer Satisfaction and Loyalty

This chapter focuses on the importance of tracking and evaluating customer satisfaction levels to gauge their loyalty and overall experience. It delves into various metrics and methods for measuring customer satisfaction, such as customer satisfaction surveys and Net Promoter Score (NPS). The chapter also emphasizes the significance of analyzing customer feedback, identifying trends, and extracting valuable insights to improve products, services, and processes. By effectively measuring and monitoring customer satisfaction and loyalty, businesses can make informed decisions and implement strategies that foster long-term customer loyalty and drive business growth.

• Key metrics for measuring customer satisfaction and loyalty

Measuring customer satisfaction and loyalty is crucial for businesses to understand the effectiveness of their customer service efforts and identify areas for improvement. This chapter explores key metrics that organizations can utilize to gauge customer satisfaction and loyalty.

One widely used metric is the Net Promoter Score (NPS), which measures customer loyalty by asking a simple question: "On a scale of 0 to 10, how likely are you to recommend our product/service to a friend or colleague?" Based on the responses, customers are classified as promoters, passives, or detractors. Calculating the NPS provides businesses with an overall view of customer loyalty and serves as a benchmark for monitoring progress over time.

Another important metric is customer satisfaction (CSAT), which measures how satisfied customers are with a specific product, service, or interaction. It typically involves asking customers to rate their satisfaction on a scale or provide feedback on specific aspects of their experience. CSAT surveys help organizations pinpoint areas of strength and weakness, allowing them to make targeted improvements to enhance overall customer satisfaction.

Customer retention rate is another vital metric that indicates the percentage of customers who continue doing business with a company over a given period. It demonstrates the level of loyalty and satisfaction among customers. A high retention rate is a positive sign of customer loyalty, while a low rate may indicate the need for improvement in customer experience or service delivery.

The Customer Effort Score (CES) measures the ease with which customers can resolve their issues or complete a task. It focuses on minimizing customer effort and streamlining processes to provide a seamless experience. By monitoring CES, businesses can identify areas where customers encounter friction and work towards simplifying those touchpoints.

Other metrics to consider include customer lifetime value (CLV), which calculates the total revenue generated from a customer throughout their relationship with the company, and customer churn rate, which measures the percentage of customers who discontinue their relationship with the company. These metrics provide insights into the long-term value of customers and help identify strategies to reduce churn and maximize customer retention.

By understanding and tracking these key metrics, businesses can gain valuable insights into customer satisfaction and loyalty. These metrics serve as indicators of the overall health of customer relationships and provide actionable data for organizations to make informed decisions, improve customer experiences, and drive business growth.

•Implementing customer satisfaction surveys and Net Promoter Score (NPS)

Implementing customer satisfaction surveys and utilizing the Net Promoter Score (NPS) are crucial steps for businesses to assess and improve customer satisfaction levels. Customer satisfaction surveys provide valuable insights into customer perceptions, preferences, and experiences, enabling organizations to identify areas of strength and areas for improvement.

To implement customer satisfaction surveys effectively, businesses need to design well-structured questionnaires that capture the relevant aspects of the customer experience. These surveys can be conducted through various channels, such as email, online platforms, or even in-person interviews. The questions should cover a range of topics, including overall satisfaction, specific product or service experiences, customer service interactions, and any issues encountered.

Implementing NPS surveys involves regularly sending out the NPS question to a representative sample of customers and collecting and analyzing their responses. This metric provides an overall view of customer loyalty and serves as a benchmark for tracking changes over time. It also helps identify potential brand advocates and areas that require improvement to enhance customer satisfaction.

To ensure the effectiveness of customer satisfaction surveys and NPS implementation, businesses should pay attention to survey design, timing, and the simplicity of response options. It's important to keep the surveys concise, easy to understand, and accessible across different devices. Additionally, prompt follow-up actions should be taken based on the survey feedback, addressing any issues raised and acknowledging positive feedback.

By implementing customer satisfaction surveys and NPS, businesses can gain valuable insights into customer perceptions and loyalty. These surveys provide quantitative data that can be used to drive improvements in product offerings, customer service, and overall customer experience. By regularly monitoring and analyzing customer feedback, businesses can identify trends, uncover areas for enhancement, and make data-driven decisions to meet and exceed customer expectations.

•Using customer feedback to drive continuous improvement

Using customer feedback to drive continuous improvement is a crucial aspect of delivering exceptional customer experiences. It involves actively collecting, analyzing, and leveraging customer feedback to identify areas for enhancement and make informed decisions that align with customer needs and expectations.

The process starts with establishing effective feedback mechanisms that allow customers to easily share their opinions, suggestions, and concerns. This can be done through various channels such as surveys, feedback forms, online reviews, social media platforms, or direct customer interactions. By actively seeking feedback, businesses demonstrate their commitment to listening and valuing customer input.

Once the feedback is collected, it needs to be carefully analyzed and categorized. This helps identify recurring themes, patterns, and specific areas that require improvement. By aggregating and analyzing the feedback, businesses can gain actionable insights and a comprehensive understanding of customer sentiment.

Based on the feedback analysis, organizations can prioritize improvement initiatives and develop action plans. This may involve addressing specific pain points, enhancing product features, streamlining processes, or improving customer service interactions. The goal is to proactively respond to customer feedback and continuously iterate and refine the customer experience.

It's essential to involve key stakeholders across the organization in the feedback analysis and improvement process. This ensures cross-functional collaboration and aligns efforts towards common goals. By sharing the customer feedback insights with relevant teams, such as product development, marketing, and customer support, organizations can foster a culture of customer-centricity and collective ownership of customer satisfaction.

Furthermore, using customer feedback as a basis for decision-making helps businesses make data-driven choices. It minimizes the risk of making assumptions and enables organizations to prioritize improvements that have the greatest impact on customer satisfaction and loyalty.

Implementing a closed-loop feedback system is another effective way to drive continuous improvement. This involves acknowledging and responding to customers' feedback, whether positive or negative. By promptly addressing concerns and sharing updates on improvements, businesses show their commitment to listening, learning, and taking action.

Leveraging customer feedback as a driver for continuous improvement empowers businesses to stay agile, adapt to changing customer needs, and consistently deliver exceptional experiences. It enables organizations to make informed decisions, foster customer loyalty, and ultimately achieve sustainable business growth.

•Analyzing customer data to identify trends and insights

Analyzing customer data to identify trends and insights

is a critical practice for businesses aiming to enhance their understanding of customer behavior, preferences, and needs. By leveraging data analytics tools and techniques, organizations can uncover valuable information that drives strategic decision-making and informs various aspects of their operations.

The first step in analyzing customer data is collecting and aggregating relevant data points from various sources such as customer interactions, transactions, surveys, website analytics, social media platforms, and more. This comprehensive dataset provides a holistic view of customer behavior and enables organizations to identify patterns, correlations, and trends.

Once the data is collected, businesses can apply statistical analysis and data visualization techniques to uncover insights. This involves employing statistical models, data mining algorithms, and machine learning approaches to identify hidden patterns or relationships within the data. By exploring correlations and associations, organizations can gain a deeper understanding of customer preferences, purchase behaviors, and engagement patterns.

Data visualization tools play a crucial role in simplifying

complex data sets into visually appealing and intuitive representations. Graphs, charts, and dashboards allow businesses to communicate insights effectively, making it easier for stakeholders to comprehend and act upon the information. Visualizations can highlight trends, outliers, and patterns that might otherwise be challenging to identify.

Analyzing customer data also involves segmenting customers based on different criteria such as demographics, behavior, preferences, or purchase history. By grouping customers into distinct segments, businesses can tailor their marketing efforts, product offerings, and customer experiences to cater to specific needs and preferences. This targeted approach increases the relevance and effectiveness of their strategies, leading to higher customer satisfaction and engagement.

In addition to segmenting customers, organizations can use data analysis to conduct customer lifetime value (CLV) analysis. CLV helps estimate the long-term value a customer brings to the business, enabling organizations to prioritize customer acquisition, retention, and loyalty initiatives accordingly. By identifying high-value customers, businesses can allocate resources effectively and develop strategies to enhance their experience and foster long-term relationships.

Analyzing customer data also facilitates predictive analytics, which involves using historical data to make informed predictions about future customer behavior. By applying predictive models, businesses can anticipate customer needs, identify potential churn risks, personalize recommendations, and optimize marketing campaigns. This proactive approach helps organizations stay ahead of customer expectations and deliver personalized experiences that drive satisfaction and loyalty.

Furthermore, data analysis allows businesses to measure and track key performance indicators (KPIs) related to customer satisfaction, retention, and loyalty. By regularly monitoring these metrics, organizations can evaluate the effectiveness of their strategies, identify areas for improvement, and make data-driven decisions to enhance overall customer success.

In short, analyzing customer data provides businesses with valuable insights that help them understand customer behavior, preferences, and trends. By leveraging advanced analytics techniques, organizations can make informed decisions, personalize customer experiences, optimize marketing efforts, and drive long-term customer satisfaction and loyalty. It enables businesses to stay competitive in a rapidly evolving marketplace and deliver exceptional value to their customers.

Chapter 13: Emotional Intelligence in Customer Relationships

This chapter explores the crucial role of emotional intelligence in building strong and meaningful connections with customers. It delves into the understanding and management of emotions, both from the customer's perspective and the service provider's standpoint. This chapter emphasizes the significance of empathy, emotional awareness, and effective communication in creating positive customer experiences. It provides strategies for developing emotional intelligence skills, managing customer emotions, and fostering strong emotional connections that lead to increased customer satisfaction, loyalty, and advocacy. By harnessing emotional intelligence, businesses can elevate their customer relationships to new heights and achieve remarkable success in today's competitive landscape.

- Understanding emotional intelligence and its impact on customer interactions

Understanding emotional intelligence is paramount when it comes to building successful customer relationships. Emotional intelligence refers to the ability to recognize, understand, and manage our own emotions, as well as the emotions of others. In the context of customer interactions, emotional intelligence plays a crucial role in how businesses engage and connect with their customers.

When service providers possess a high level of emotional intelligence, they are better equipped to understand and empathize with customer emotions. They can effectively recognize and interpret the emotional cues expressed by customers, allowing them to respond appropriately and provide the necessary support. This understanding helps in creating a positive and personalized customer experience.

Emotional intelligence also enables service providers to regulate their own emotions during customer interactions. By managing their own emotions, they can remain calm, composed, and empathetic, even in challenging situations. This emotional regulation helps in diffusing tense situations and finding mutually beneficial solutions.

Moreover, emotional intelligence enhances communication skills, allowing service providers to effectively convey empathy, understanding, and care to customers. They can actively listen to customer concerns, validate their emotions, and provide clear and empathetic responses. This level of communication builds trust and rapport with customers, making them feel valued and understood.

The impact of emotional intelligence on customer interactions is profound. Customers are more likely to remember and appreciate positive emotional experiences. They feel a stronger connection to the brand or organization that prioritizes their emotional well-being. This positive emotional connection leads to increased customer satisfaction, loyalty, and advocacy.

In contrast, a lack of emotional intelligence can result in negative customer experiences. Service providers who struggle to understand or manage emotions may respond insensitively or fail to meet customer needs. This can lead to frustration, disappointment, and ultimately, a breakdown in the customer relationship.

By understanding the importance of emotional intelligence and its impact on customer interactions, businesses can train and develop their employees to enhance their emotional intelligence skills. This can be done through training programs, workshops, and ongoing coaching. The result is a team of service providers who are emotionally attuned, responsive, and capable of delivering exceptional customer experiences.

•Developing empathy and emotional awareness in customer service

Developing empathy and emotional awareness in customer service is crucial for fostering meaningful and impactful interactions with customers. Empathy is the ability to understand and share the feelings of others, while emotional awareness refers to the capacity to recognize and understand one's own emotions. By cultivating these skills, service providers can create a more empathetic and customer-centric experience.

Empathy allows service providers to put themselves in the customer's shoes and truly understand their perspective. It involves actively listening to their concerns, validating their emotions, and showing genuine care and understanding. When service providers demonstrate empathy, it helps to establish a sense of trust and connection with the customer, leading to a more positive and satisfying experience.

Emotional awareness, on the other hand, involves being in tune with one's own emotions. By understanding their own emotional state, service providers can better manage and regulate their responses during customer interactions. This awareness enables them to remain calm and composed, even in challenging situations, and respond in a way that is helpful and empathetic.

Developing empathy and emotional awareness requires self-reflection and practice. Service providers can benefit from training programs and workshops that focus on emotional intelligence and empathy-building techniques. These programs help individuals develop their ability to recognize and understand emotions, both in themselves and in others. They also provide practical strategies for expressing empathy, such as active listening, using empathetic language, and responding to customer emotions with care and compassion.

Fostering a culture of empathy within the organization is essential. When empathy is valued and encouraged from the top down, it becomes ingrained in the organization's customer service approach. This can be achieved through leadership support, employee recognition for demonstrating empathy, and incorporating empathy into the organization's values and mission.

By developing empathy and emotional awareness in customer service, organizations can create an environment where customers feel heard, understood, and supported. This leads to enhanced customer satisfaction, loyalty, and advocacy. Additionally, it contributes to a positive and inclusive workplace culture, as employees are encouraged to connect with customers on a deeper, more empathetic level.

Developing empathy and emotional awareness in customer service is a fundamental aspect of providing exceptional customer experiences. It empowers service providers to connect with customers on an emotional level, understand their needs and concerns, and respond in a compassionate and supportive manner.

•Managing and defusing customer emotions effectively

Managing and defusing customer emotions effectively is an essential skill for customer service professionals. Customer emotions can range from frustration and anger to disappointment and confusion, and it's crucial to handle these emotions in a way that resolves the issue and maintains a positive customer experience.

One key aspect of managing customer emotions is active listening. By actively listening to the customer's concerns and allowing them to express their emotions, service providers demonstrate empathy and create a safe space for the customer to vent their frustrations. It's important to let customers feel heard and validated, acknowledging their emotions without judgment.

In addition to active listening, it's important to remain calm and composed when faced with intense customer emotions. Service providers should avoid becoming defensive or argumentative, as this can escalate the situation further. Instead, they should adopt a patient and understanding approach, showing empathy and reassurance to the customer.

To effectively defuse customer emotions, service providers can utilize various techniques. One approach is to reframe the situation and focus on finding a solution rather than dwelling on the problem. Offering alternatives or suggesting compromises can help alleviate the customer's negative emotions and shift the conversation towards resolution.

Another effective technique is to practice effective communication. Using clear and concise language, service providers can explain the steps being taken to address the issue and provide a timeline for resolution. This helps manage the customer's expectations and reassures them that their concerns are being taken seriously.

Empowering customers by involving them in the problem-solving process can also help defuse emotions. This can include seeking their input, asking for their suggestions, and keeping them informed about the progress being made. By involving customers in the resolution, they feel valued and regain a sense of control over the situation, which can lead to a more positive emotional response.

Training programs and workshops can help customer service professionals develop their skills in managing and defusing customer emotions. These programs provide insights into emotional intelligence, effective communication techniques, and conflict resolution strategies. By enhancing their emotional intelligence and communication skills, service providers are better equipped to handle challenging customer interactions.

By effectively managing and defusing customer emotions, organizations can turn potential negative experiences into positive ones. When customers feel that their emotions are acknowledged and addressed, they are more likely to remain loyal and speak positively about their experiences. It also contributes to the overall reputation and customer satisfaction of the organization, fostering stronger relationships and long-term success.

•Building strong emotional connections with customers

Building strong emotional connections with customers is a crucial aspect of customer relationship management. When customers feel emotionally connected to a brand or company, they are more likely to develop loyalty, engage in repeat purchases, and become advocates for the brand.

One way to build emotional connections is through personalized and meaningful interactions. By understanding and acknowledging customers' individual needs, preferences, and values, companies can tailor their interactions to create a sense of empathy and care. This can be achieved through personalized communication, remembering and referencing previous interactions, and offering customized solutions to meet specific needs.

Another effective strategy is to create positive and memorable experiences for customers. By going above and beyond in delivering exceptional service or surprising customers with unexpected gestures, companies can evoke positive emotions and leave a lasting impression. These experiences can include personalized thank-you notes, special promotions or discounts, or exclusive access to events or content.

Consistency in delivering high-quality experiences is also important in building emotional connections. When customers consistently receive exceptional service and support, they develop a sense of trust and reliability towards the brand. This consistency builds a foundation for a strong emotional bond and establishes the brand as a reliable partner in meeting their needs.

Active listening and empathy play a significant role in building emotional connections. By truly understanding and empathizing with customers' concerns, challenges, and aspirations, companies can demonstrate their commitment to their customers' success and well-being. This can be achieved through effective communication, showing genuine interest, and offering empathetic responses to customer feedback or issues.

Storytelling is another powerful tool in building emotional connections. Sharing authentic and relatable stories that resonate with customers can evoke emotions and create a sense of shared values and experiences. Whether through testimonials, case studies, or brand narratives, storytelling humanizes the brand and creates a deeper connection with customers.

Fostering a sense of community and belonging can strengthen emotional connections. By creating opportunities for customers to connect with each other and the brand, such as online communities, forums, or events, companies can facilitate meaningful interactions and create a sense of belonging. This fosters a sense of loyalty and emotional attachment, as customers feel part of a larger community that shares common values and experiences.

Building strong emotional connections with customers requires understanding their needs, providing personalized experiences, demonstrating empathy and active listening, and fostering a sense of community. By investing in building emotional connections, companies can cultivate long-term relationships, drive customer loyalty, and differentiate themselves in a competitive marketplace.

Chapter 14: Managing Customer Expectations

This chapter focuses on the importance of setting and managing realistic expectations to ensure customer satisfaction. By understanding customer expectations and aligning them with the capabilities of the product or service, businesses can enhance the overall customer experience. This chapter explores strategies for effective communication, managing expectations throughout the customer journey, and handling situations where expectations cannot be met. It emphasizes the significance of transparency, clear communication, and proactive management of customer expectations to build trust, avoid misunderstandings, and deliver on promises. By effectively managing expectations, businesses can foster stronger customer relationships and drive long-term loyalty.

- Setting realistic expectations through transparent communication

Setting realistic expectations through transparent communication is a crucial aspect of delivering exceptional customer experiences. This involves ensuring that customers have a clear understanding of what they can expect from a product or service. Transparent communication helps build trust, fosters positive relationships, and avoids misunderstandings or disappointments.

To set realistic expectations, businesses must provide accurate and honest information about their offerings. This includes sharing details about product features, limitations, pricing, delivery timelines, and any potential challenges or risks. By being transparent, businesses demonstrate their commitment to integrity and customer-centricity.

Transparent communication also involves actively listening to customers and addressing their concerns or questions. It requires open and honest dialogue, where businesses provide clear explanations and manage customer expectations based on the available resources and capabilities. This helps avoid overpromising and underdelivering, which can lead to dissatisfaction and negative experiences.

Furthermore, businesses should be proactive in managing expectations throughout the customer journey. This means providing regular updates on progress, notifying customers of any changes or delays, and promptly addressing any issues that may arise. By keeping customers informed and involved, businesses foster a sense of trust and reliability.

When setting expectations, it is essential to strike a balance between meeting customer desires and maintaining feasibility. While it is important to strive for excellence, it is equally crucial to ensure that expectations are achievable within the boundaries of the product or service. By setting realistic expectations, businesses avoid creating false hopes and prevent customer disappointment.

Transparent communication also plays a role in managing customer complaints or escalations. By being upfront and transparent about the steps being taken to address the issue, businesses can alleviate customer concerns and rebuild trust. Transparent communication demonstrates empathy and shows that the business values the customer's perspective.

In summary, setting realistic expectations through transparent communication is vital for building trust, managing customer relationships, and delivering exceptional experiences. By providing accurate information, actively listening to customers, and proactively managing expectations, businesses can create a solid foundation for positive customer interactions and long-term loyalty.

•Managing customer expectations during the sales and onboarding process

Managing customer expectations during the sales and onboarding process is crucial for building strong customer relationships and ensuring a smooth transition into using a product or service. This involves effectively communicating the features, benefits, and limitations of the offering to align customer expectations with the actual experience.

During the sales process, businesses must provide clear and accurate information about the product or service. This includes outlining its capabilities, functionalities, and any potential constraints or requirements. By being transparent about what the offering can and cannot do, businesses set realistic expectations and avoid any potential mismatch between customer expectations and the actual capabilities of the product or service.

Additionally, businesses should manage customer expectations by addressing any concerns or questions during the onboarding process. This includes providing comprehensive documentation, tutorials, or training sessions to help customers understand how to effectively use the product or service. By proactively assisting customers in navigating the initial stages of adoption, businesses set the stage for a positive customer experience and minimize any potential frustration or confusion.

Managing customer expectations also involves being transparent about timelines and deliverables. Providing accurate estimates for implementation, delivery, or resolution of any outstanding issues helps customers understand what to expect and when. This transparency promotes trust and demonstrates the business's commitment to meeting customer needs.

Moreover, businesses should actively communicate any changes or updates that may impact the customer's experience. Whether it's a new feature release, a change in pricing, or a shift in policies, timely and transparent communication ensures that customers are aware of any adjustments and can adjust their expectations accordingly.

Throughout the sales and onboarding process, businesses must actively listen to customer feedback and address any concerns promptly. By promptly addressing customer issues and providing effective solutions, businesses demonstrate their commitment to customer satisfaction and reinforce their reputation for excellent service.

By effectively managing customer expectations during the sales and onboarding process, businesses lay the foundation for a positive customer experience. Transparent communication, accurate information, and proactive assistance contribute to building trust, fostering customer satisfaction, and facilitating a seamless transition into using the product or service.

•Addressing and exceeding customer expectations through consistent delivery

Addressing and exceeding customer expectations through consistent delivery is a crucial aspect of building strong customer relationships and fostering customer satisfaction. It involves aligning the delivery of products or services with the promises made during the sales and onboarding process, and consistently meeting or surpassing customer expectations throughout the entire customer journey.

To address customer expectations, businesses must ensure that the core features, functionalities, and benefits promised to customers are consistently delivered. This requires careful planning, effective execution, and quality control measures to ensure that the product or service performs as expected and meets the customer's needs.

Exceeding customer expectations goes beyond meeting the basic requirements and aims to provide additional value and exceptional experiences. This can be achieved by going the extra mile to personalize the customer experience, offering additional features or benefits, or providing exceptional customer service.

Consistency is key in addressing and exceeding customer expectations. Customers rely on businesses to deliver a consistent experience every time they interact with the brand. This means delivering products or services that consistently meet the promised standards, adhering to agreed-upon timelines, and providing consistent levels of quality and support.

Businesses can also strive to exceed customer expectations by anticipating their needs and proactively offering solutions or recommendations. By understanding their customers' preferences, pain points, and challenges, businesses can provide tailored recommendations, suggest relevant products or services, or offer customized solutions to address their specific needs.

To ensure consistent delivery and exceed customer expectations, businesses should regularly monitor and measure customer satisfaction levels, gather feedback, and make necessary improvements. This feedback loop helps businesses identify areas for improvement and adjust their processes or offerings to better meet customer needs.

By consistently addressing and exceeding customer expectations, businesses can build trust, loyalty, and advocacy. Customers appreciate when their expectations are not only met but exceeded, and they are more likely to become repeat customers and recommend the business to others.

Addressing and exceeding customer expectations through consistent delivery involves delivering on the promises made during the sales process, consistently meeting customer needs and preferences, and going above and beyond to provide exceptional experiences. By focusing on customer satisfaction and continuously improving, businesses can establish a reputation for exceeding customer expectations and build long-lasting customer relationships.

•Handling situations where expectations cannot be met

Handling situations where expectations cannot be met is a crucial aspect of managing customer relationships and ensuring customer satisfaction. It involves effectively communicating with customers, managing their disappointment or frustration, and finding alternative solutions to address their needs or concerns.

When a business realizes that it cannot meet a customer's expectations, it is important to be transparent and honest in communication. Clearly explain the limitations or constraints that prevent the expectations from being met, and offer a sincere apology for any inconvenience caused. This helps to manage the customer's disappointment and build trust by demonstrating integrity and accountability.

During such situations, active listening is essential. Allow the customer to express their concerns and emotions, and show empathy towards their disappointment. Acknowledge their feelings and validate their perspective, which helps to defuse tension and foster a constructive dialogue.

To effectively handle unmet expectations, it is crucial to offer alternative solutions or options whenever possible. This may involve exploring alternative products, services, or delivery methods that can still meet the customer's needs or objectives. Collaborate with the customer to find a mutually acceptable solution that aligns with their expectations and your business capabilities.

In some cases, it may not be possible to provide a direct solution that meets the customer's original expectations. In such situations, it is important to focus on finding a compromise or offering additional value to mitigate their disappointment. This can include providing discounts, refunds, or other incentives as a gesture of goodwill and to preserve the customer's trust and satisfaction.

It is essential to learn from these situations and implement improvements in the future. Analyze the reasons behind the unmet expectations and identify areas for process or product/service enhancement. By using this feedback to drive continuous improvement, businesses can minimize similar instances in the future and better manage customer expectations.

Handling situations where expectations cannot be met requires effective communication, empathy, and a proactive approach to finding alternative solutions. By managing these situations professionally and finding ways to address customer needs and concerns, businesses can mitigate the negative impact and maintain positive customer relationships.

Chapter 15: Building a Customer-Centric Culture

This chapter focuses on the importance of fostering a customer-centric mindset throughout an organization. It explores strategies for aligning departments and functions to prioritize customer satisfaction and loyalty. The chapter emphasizes the need for empowering employees to become customer advocates and highlights the benefits of cross-functional collaboration. It delves into the development of a customer-centric organizational culture that places customers at the center of decision-making processes and encourages a strong focus on delivering exceptional customer experiences. By building a customer-centric culture, businesses can create a sustainable competitive advantage and establish long-lasting relationships with their customers.

- Aligning departments and functions to deliver exceptional customer experiences

Aligning departments and functions to deliver exceptional customer experiences is a critical aspect of building a customer-centric organization. This involves breaking down silos and fostering collaboration among different departments to ensure a seamless and consistent customer journey across all touchpoints.

Firstly, it requires clear communication and shared goals across departments. By aligning everyone towards a common objective of delivering exceptional customer experiences, organizations can create a unified approach that puts the customer at the center of decision-making.

Secondly, it involves creating cross-functional teams or task forces that bring together representatives from different departments. These teams can work collaboratively to identify customer pain points, streamline processes, and implement improvements that enhance the overall customer experience. By leveraging the expertise and insights from various departments, organizations can address customer needs more effectively and efficiently.

Thirdly, organizations need to establish effective communication channels and systems to facilitate the sharing of customer feedback and insights across departments. This ensures that everyone has access to the same customer data and can make informed decisions based on a holistic understanding of customer preferences, challenges, and expectations.

Moreover, it is essential to establish clear roles and responsibilities for each department in delivering exceptional customer experiences. This includes defining key performance indicators (KPIs) that measure the impact of each department's efforts on the overall customer experience. By aligning departmental goals with customer satisfaction metrics, organizations can incentivize and motivate employees to prioritize customer-centric actions.

Regular cross-departmental meetings and workshops can be conducted to foster collaboration, share best practices, and identify areas for improvement. These interactions provide opportunities for different departments to learn from each other, leverage each other's strengths, and find innovative solutions to enhance the customer experience.

By aligning departments and functions to deliver exceptional customer experiences, organizations can create a culture of customer-centricity that permeates throughout the entire organization. This alignment not only improves the customer journey but also enhances internal collaboration and efficiency. Ultimately, it allows organizations to differentiate themselves from competitors and build long-term relationships with customers based on trust, satisfaction, and loyalty.

• Empowering employees to become customer advocates

Empowering employees to become customer advocates is a crucial aspect of fostering a customer-centric culture within an organization. When employees are empowered, they become actively engaged in delivering exceptional customer experiences and act as ambassadors for the organization.

Firstly, empowering employees involves providing them with the necessary training and resources to understand the importance of customer advocacy and develop the skills needed to excel in customer interactions. This includes training programs that focus on enhancing communication, problem-solving, and empathy skills. By equipping employees with the right tools and knowledge, they are better prepared to serve customers effectively and represent the organization positively.

Secondly, organizations need to foster a supportive and inclusive work environment that encourages employee engagement and ownership. This can be achieved through open communication channels, regular feedback sessions, and recognition programs that celebrate employee contributions. When employees feel valued and supported, they are more likely to take pride in their work and go above and beyond to satisfy customer needs.

Organizations can empower employees by giving them autonomy and decision-making authority to resolve customer issues. By empowering front-line employees to make decisions that benefit the customer, organizations demonstrate trust in their capabilities and foster a sense of accountability. This, in turn, enables employees to respond promptly and effectively to customer concerns, leading to improved customer satisfaction and loyalty.

Additionally, organizations can create a culture of continuous learning and improvement, where employees are encouraged to share customer insights and innovative ideas. By providing platforms for employees to contribute their knowledge and experiences, organizations tap into a wealth of valuable information that can drive customer-centric initiatives and improvements.

Recognizing and rewarding employees for their customer-centric efforts further reinforces the importance of customer advocacy. This can be done through performance-based incentives, peer recognition programs, or even internal awards that highlight exceptional customer service achievements. Recognizing and celebrating employee contributions not only motivates individuals but also inspires others to embody the same customer-centric mindset.

By empowering employees to become customer advocates, organizations cultivate a workforce that is committed to delivering outstanding customer experiences. These empowered employees become ambassadors for the organization, promoting its values and brand reputation. Ultimately, this leads to increased customer satisfaction, loyalty, and positive word-of-mouth, contributing to the overall success and growth of the organization.

•Fostering a customer-centric mindset and values throughout the organization

Fostering a customer-centric mindset and values throughout the organization is crucial for creating a culture that prioritizes and embraces the needs and preferences of customers. It involves instilling a shared belief and commitment to delivering exceptional customer experiences at every touchpoint.

To foster a customer-centric mindset, organizations need to emphasize the importance of customer satisfaction and loyalty as key drivers of success. This can be done through regular communication and training sessions that highlight the significance of customer-centricity and its impact on business outcomes.

Leadership plays a crucial role in fostering a customer-centric mindset by setting the example and modeling customer-centric behaviors. When leaders demonstrate a genuine dedication to customer satisfaction and prioritize customer needs in decision-making processes, it sends a strong message throughout the organization.

Organizations also need to ensure that customer-centric values are embedded in their core values and mission statement. By explicitly stating their commitment to customer satisfaction and incorporating it into the organization's DNA, it becomes a guiding principle for all employees.

To foster a customer-centric culture, organizations should create clear customer service standards and expectations that are communicated to all employees. This involves defining and articulating the desired customer experience and ensuring that all employees understand their role in delivering it.

Training programs and workshops focused on customer-centric skills and behaviors can be implemented to provide employees with the necessary tools and knowledge. This includes skills such as active listening, empathy, problem-solving, and effective communication, which are essential for delivering exceptional customer experiences.

In addition, organizations can establish regular feedback mechanisms and platforms for employees to share customer insights and suggestions. This allows employees to feel heard and valued, while also providing valuable information to drive customer-centric improvements and innovations.

Recognizing and rewarding employees who consistently demonstrate customer-centric behaviors is another effective way to foster a customer-centric mindset. By acknowledging and celebrating employees who go above and beyond to satisfy customer needs, organizations reinforce the importance of customer-centricity and motivate others to follow suit.

By fostering a customer-centric mindset and values throughout the organization, businesses create a culture that consistently delivers exceptional customer experiences. This not only leads to increased customer satisfaction, loyalty, and advocacy but also sets the organization apart from competitors and contributes to long-term success and growth.

•Encouraging cross-functional collaboration for enhanced customer focus

Encouraging cross-functional collaboration is essential for enhancing customer focus within an organization. It involves breaking down silos and fostering teamwork and communication across different departments and functions to ensure a seamless and consistent customer experience.

Cross-functional collaboration brings together individuals from various teams, such as sales, marketing, customer service, product development, and operations, to work collectively towards a common goal of delivering exceptional customer value. By leveraging the diverse expertise and perspectives of each department, organizations can gain a holistic understanding of customer needs and preferences.

To encourage cross-functional collaboration, organizations can create platforms and opportunities for teams to come together and share insights, ideas, and best practices. Regular meetings, workshops, and brainstorming sessions can facilitate open communication and collaboration, allowing teams to align their efforts and work towards a shared customer-centric vision.

Clear communication channels and effective collaboration tools can also be implemented to streamline communication and foster collaboration among different departments. This ensures that information flows smoothly, enabling teams to collaborate on projects, address customer issues, and coordinate efforts more efficiently.

Cross-functional collaboration also promotes a sense of ownership and accountability for the customer experience. When teams work together, they understand the impact of their actions on the overall customer journey and take collective responsibility for delivering exceptional experiences.

Encouraging cross-functional collaboration can also lead to innovation and continuous improvement. By bringing together diverse perspectives and expertise, teams can identify opportunities for process optimization, product enhancements, and service improvements. This collaborative approach allows organizations to adapt quickly to evolving customer needs and stay ahead of the competition.

Cross-functional collaboration helps break down internal barriers and promotes a customer-centric culture throughout the organization. When teams work together towards a common goal of customer satisfaction, it fosters a shared understanding and commitment to putting customers at the center of decision-making and actions.

Encouraging cross-functional collaboration is vital for enhancing customer focus within an organization. By fostering teamwork, communication, and knowledge sharing among different departments, organizations can ensure a seamless customer experience, drive innovation, and create a customer-centric culture that sets them apart in today's competitive landscape.

Chapter 16: Innovation and Adaptability in Customer Service

This chapter explores the importance of innovation and adaptability in delivering exceptional customer service. It highlights the need for organizations to embrace new ideas, technologies, and approaches to meet evolving customer expectations. By fostering a culture of innovation, businesses can identify opportunities for improvement, implement creative solutions, and stay ahead of the competition. The chapter emphasizes the importance of adapting to changing customer needs, preferences, and market dynamics. It also explores how organizations can leverage emerging technologies and adopt agile methodologies to enhance customer service and drive continuous improvement. Ultimately, the chapter empowers businesses to embrace innovation and adaptability as key drivers of customer satisfaction and business success.

- Embracing innovation in customer service and experience design

Embracing innovation in customer service and experience design is crucial for businesses to stay competitive in today's rapidly evolving market. It involves adopting new technologies, strategies, and approaches to enhance the overall customer experience and meet their changing expectations.

One aspect of embracing innovation is leveraging digital advancements. This includes implementing chatbots, virtual assistants, and self-service portals to provide customers with quick and efficient support. By offering these self-help options, businesses can empower customers to find solutions on their own, reducing the need for traditional customer support channels.

In addition, businesses can utilize data analytics and artificial intelligence to gain valuable insights into customer behavior and preferences. By analyzing customer data, businesses can identify patterns, trends, and pain points, enabling them to personalize the customer experience and offer relevant and targeted solutions. This level of personalization enhances customer satisfaction and loyalty.

Another aspect of innovation in customer service is the use of omnichannel communication. Customers expect a seamless experience across various channels, whether it's through a website, mobile app, social media, or in-person interactions. By integrating these channels and providing a consistent experience, businesses can improve customer engagement and satisfaction.

Businesses can embrace innovation by adopting agile methodologies and design thinking principles. This involves involving customers in the product development process, gathering their feedback, and iterating on solutions to ensure they meet customer needs. By continuously testing and improving their products and services based on customer feedback, businesses can stay ahead of the competition and deliver exceptional customer experiences.

Lastly, embracing innovation requires a culture that encourages and rewards creativity and risk-taking. It involves empowering employees to think outside the box, experiment with new ideas, and challenge the status quo. By fostering a culture of innovation, businesses can tap into the collective knowledge and expertise of their workforce to drive continuous improvement and deliver innovative solutions.

Embracing innovation in customer service and experience design is essential for businesses to meet the evolving needs and expectations of customers. By leveraging technology, data analytics, omnichannel communication, and adopting agile methodologies, businesses can enhance the customer experience, increase satisfaction, and gain a competitive edge in the market. Embracing innovation is not just about keeping up with the latest trends but also about proactively seeking opportunities to improve and create value for customers.

•Adopting emerging technologies to enhance customer interactions

Adopting emerging technologies to enhance customer interactions is a crucial aspect of staying competitive in today's digital age. As technology continues to advance at a rapid pace, businesses need to embrace these innovations to meet the evolving expectations of their customers.

One way businesses can adopt emerging technologies is through the integration of artificial intelligence (AI) and machine learning (ML) into their customer service processes. AI-powered chatbots and virtual assistants can provide instant and personalized responses to customer queries, improving response times and overall customer satisfaction. These technologies can handle routine tasks, freeing up human agents to focus on more complex issues.

Another emerging technology that can enhance customer interactions is the Internet of Things (IoT). By connecting physical devices and objects to the internet, businesses can collect valuable data and provide personalized experiences. For example, IoT devices in retail stores can track customer preferences and behavior to offer targeted promotions and recommendations. In the hospitality industry, IoT-enabled devices can create a seamless and personalized guest experience by adjusting room settings based on individual preferences.

Businesses can leverage augmented reality (AR) and virtual reality (VR) technologies to create immersive and engaging customer experiences. AR can be used to provide real-time product information or overlay digital content onto physical environments, while VR can transport customers to virtual environments for interactive experiences. These technologies can be especially valuable in industries such as retail, tourism, and real estate.

Additionally, the adoption of voice-activated

technology, such as voice assistants and smart speakers, is gaining popularity. Customers can interact with these devices using natural language, allowing for hands-free and convenient interactions. Businesses can integrate voice-activated technology into their customer service processes, making it easier for customers to access information and make inquiries.

Lastly, blockchain technology offers opportunities for enhancing customer interactions, particularly in areas such as supply chain management and security. Blockchain's decentralized and transparent nature can improve trust and traceability, ensuring customers have confidence in the authenticity and integrity of products and services.

Adopting emerging technologies is essential for businesses to enhance customer interactions and meet their ever-changing expectations. By leveraging AI, IoT, AR/VR, voice-activated technology, and blockchain, businesses can provide personalized, immersive, and convenient experiences. Embracing these technologies not only improves customer satisfaction but also enables businesses to gain a competitive edge in the digital marketplace.

•Encouraging a culture of experimentation and learning from customer feedback

Encouraging a culture of experimentation and learning from customer feedback is essential for businesses to stay innovative and continuously improve their products and services. It involves creating an environment where employees are empowered to take risks, explore new ideas, and adapt based on customer insights.

By fostering a culture of experimentation, businesses can encourage employees to think outside the box and try new approaches. This mindset allows for the exploration of different strategies, processes, and technologies that can lead to breakthrough innovations. Employees are encouraged to take calculated risks and learn from both successes and failures, understanding that failures are valuable opportunities for growth and learning.

One way to promote experimentation is by allocating resources and time specifically for innovation projects. This could involve setting aside a portion of the budget for research and development, providing dedicated time for employees to work on innovation initiatives, or creating cross-functional teams to collaborate on new ideas. By creating these opportunities, businesses signal their commitment to experimentation and provide a safe space for employees to explore new concepts.

Learning from customer feedback is another crucial aspect of a culture of experimentation. Businesses should actively seek and listen to customer insights to understand their needs, preferences, and pain points. This feedback can come from various sources, such as customer surveys, social media interactions, customer support interactions, and online reviews.

Once customer feedback is collected, it is important to analyze and extract valuable insights. Businesses can use data analytics tools to identify patterns and trends, uncover areas for improvement, and make data-driven decisions. By understanding customer feedback, businesses can make informed adjustments to their products, services, and customer experiences.

It is essential to foster a learning mindset within the organization. This involves encouraging employees to continuously seek knowledge, stay updated on industry trends, and engage in professional development activities. Businesses can facilitate learning by providing training programs, mentorship opportunities, and resources for employees to expand their skills and knowledge.

Overall, encouraging a culture of experimentation and learning from customer feedback promotes innovation, agility, and customer-centricity. It allows businesses to stay ahead of the competition, anticipate customer needs, and deliver exceptional experiences. By embracing experimentation and valuing customer insights, businesses can continuously evolve and adapt to meet the ever-changing demands of their customers.

•Adapting to changing customer needs and market dynamics

Adapting to changing customer needs and market dynamics is crucial for businesses to remain competitive and relevant in today's fast-paced and ever-evolving marketplace. It involves recognizing shifts in customer preferences, behaviors, and expectations, and proactively adjusting strategies, products, and services to meet those changing demands.

One of the key aspects of adapting to changing customer needs is staying attuned to customer feedback and market trends. This includes actively listening to customer insights, conducting market research, and monitoring industry developments. By understanding the evolving needs and preferences of customers, businesses can identify opportunities for innovation and make informed decisions about product development, enhancements, and marketing strategies.

Flexibility is another important factor in adapting to changing customer needs. Businesses must be willing to adjust their operations, processes, and offerings in response to shifts in the market. This may involve revisiting business models, exploring new distribution channels, or introducing new features or services. By being open to change and embracing agility, businesses can stay ahead of the curve and ensure their offerings remain relevant and valuable to customers.

Collaboration and communication within the organization are essential for successful adaptation. Different departments and teams should share information and insights to foster a holistic understanding of customer needs and market dynamics. This collaborative approach enables businesses to respond quickly to changes and make coordinated decisions that align with the evolving landscape.

Technology plays a crucial role in adapting to changing customer needs as well. By leveraging technological advancements, businesses can streamline processes, improve efficiency, and deliver personalized experiences. For example, utilizing customer relationship management (CRM) systems, data analytics tools, and automation can enable businesses to gather and analyze customer data, identify patterns, and tailor their offerings accordingly.

Fostering a culture of innovation and continuous improvement is essential for adapting to changing customer needs. Encouraging employees to think creatively, take risks, and embrace change cultivates an environment that is receptive to new ideas and solutions. It also empowers employees to contribute their insights and suggestions for enhancing products and services to better meet customer expectations.

Adapting to changing customer needs and market dynamics is a fundamental aspect of business success. By staying attentive to customer feedback, remaining flexible, fostering collaboration, leveraging technology, and fostering a culture of innovation, businesses can effectively respond to evolving customer demands and thrive in a competitive marketplace.

Chapter 17: Leveraging Technology for Customer Success

This chapter explores the role of technology in driving customer success and satisfaction. It delves into the various tools, platforms, and applications that businesses can utilize to enhance customer experiences, streamline processes, and gather valuable insights. From customer relationship management (CRM) systems to automation and artificial intelligence (AI), this chapter highlights the benefits and best practices of leveraging technology in managing customer relationships and ensuring their success. It also emphasizes the importance of striking a balance between technological advancements and maintaining a human touch in customer interactions, ultimately leading to improved customer retention, loyalty, and business growth.

•Exploring customer relationship management (CRM) systems and tools

Customer relationship management (CRM) systems and tools are essential components in managing and optimizing customer relationships. These systems provide businesses with a centralized platform to store and analyze customer data, track interactions, and streamline communication. By exploring CRM systems and tools, businesses gain valuable insights into their customers' preferences, behaviors, and purchase history, enabling them to tailor their approach and deliver personalized experiences.

CRM systems offer a range of functionalities, such as contact management, sales automation, marketing automation, and customer service management. They allow businesses to efficiently manage customer information, track sales opportunities, and automate marketing campaigns. With the help of CRM tools, businesses can segment their customer base, create targeted marketing campaigns, and track the effectiveness of their marketing efforts.

CRM systems facilitate effective customer service management by providing customer support teams with access to relevant customer information, including previous interactions, inquiries, and complaints. This enables customer service representatives to provide personalized and timely assistance, resulting in enhanced customer satisfaction.

CRM systems also play a crucial role in improving

collaboration and communication across different departments within an organization. Sales teams can share customer data, track sales progress, and collaborate on strategies, ensuring a seamless customer experience throughout the entire sales process. Marketing teams can align their efforts with customer preferences and behaviors, creating more targeted and impactful campaigns. Customer service teams can access relevant customer information, allowing them to provide consistent and personalized support.

In addition, CRM systems integrate with other business tools and technologies, such as email marketing software, social media platforms, and analytics tools, further enhancing their capabilities and effectiveness. They enable businesses to leverage customer data for predictive analytics, enabling them to identify trends, anticipate customer needs, and make data-driven decisions.

Exploring CRM systems and tools is crucial for businesses aiming to optimize customer relationships. By implementing an effective CRM strategy, businesses can improve customer satisfaction, increase sales and revenue, and foster long-term customer loyalty.

•Implementing automation and AI technologies for enhanced customer experiences

Implementing automation and artificial intelligence (AI) technologies can revolutionize customer experiences by streamlining processes, personalizing interactions, and delivering exceptional service. Automation can significantly enhance efficiency and speed in customer service, sales, and marketing activities, resulting in improved overall customer experiences.

In customer service, automation tools like chatbots and virtual assistants can handle routine inquiries, provide quick responses, and assist customers. By automating simple tasks, businesses can free up their customer service agents' time to focus on more complex issues, improving response times and customer satisfaction. AI-powered chatbots can even learn from customer interactions and provide increasingly accurate and personalized responses over time.

AI technologies can also enhance sales processes by analyzing customer data and generating valuable insights. By leveraging machine learning algorithms, businesses can identify patterns and trends in customer behavior, enabling them to offer tailored product recommendations, targeted promotions, and personalized offers. AI can help sales teams prioritize leads, predict customer needs, and optimize pricing strategies for better conversions and increased revenue.

In marketing, automation and AI technologies can automate repetitive tasks such as email marketing, social media scheduling, and campaign management. By leveraging customer data and AI algorithms, businesses can create highly personalized and targeted marketing campaigns, delivering the right message to the right customer at the right time. Automation can also enable businesses to track customer interactions and behaviors, allowing for more effective lead nurturing and customer engagement.

AI-powered analytics tools can provide businesses with valuable insights into customer preferences, sentiment analysis, and predictive analytics. These insights can inform decision-making processes, enabling businesses to optimize their product offerings, identify market trends, and anticipate customer needs. AI can also help identify potential churn risks and provide recommendations for proactive retention strategies.

Implementing automation and AI technologies requires careful planning and consideration to ensure a seamless integration with existing systems and processes. It is essential to strike a balance between automation and human interaction to maintain a personalized touch and address complex customer inquiries. By leveraging automation and AI technologies, businesses can deliver enhanced customer experiences, improve operational efficiency, and gain a competitive edge in today's digital landscape.

•Utilizing chatbots and self-service portals for efficient customer support

Utilizing chatbots and self-service portals has become increasingly popular in the realm of customer support, offering businesses an efficient and convenient way to address customer inquiries and provide timely assistance. Chatbots, powered by artificial intelligence (AI), are virtual assistants that can interact with customers in real-time, answering questions, providing information, and guiding them through various processes.

Chatbots offer several advantages for customer support. They provide 24/7 availability, allowing customers to seek assistance at any time, regardless of business hours. This immediate response capability enhances customer satisfaction and reduces waiting times. Moreover, chatbots can handle multiple inquiries simultaneously, ensuring a swift and efficient resolution of customer issues.

Self-service portals, on the other hand, empower customers to find solutions to their problems independently. These portals offer a range of resources such as FAQs, knowledge bases, tutorials, and troubleshooting guides. By providing self-service options, businesses enable customers to access information and resolve simple issues on their own, without the need for direct assistance.

By leveraging chatbots and self-service portals, businesses can significantly reduce the load on their support teams, allowing them to focus on more complex customer inquiries. This not only increases the efficiency of customer support operations but also reduces costs associated with hiring additional staff or outsourcing support services.

Additionally, chatbots and self-service portals can improve the overall customer experience by providing quick and accurate responses. Chatbots can analyze customer queries and provide relevant information or route inquiries to the appropriate support channels when necessary. Self-service portals offer customers the freedom to access information at their convenience, empowering them to solve problems at their own pace.

However, it's important to note that while chatbots and self-service portals are valuable tools, they should not completely replace human interaction in customer support. There will always be cases that require the expertise and empathy of human agents. Therefore, it is essential for businesses to strike the right balance between automated assistance and human touch to ensure a seamless and personalized customer experience.

Utilizing chatbots and self-service portals for customer support offers businesses an efficient and effective way to address customer inquiries and provide timely assistance. These technologies enhance customer satisfaction, reduce waiting times, and optimize support operations, all while offering customers the convenience of self-service options. When implemented alongside human support, chatbots and self-service portals can significantly improve the overall customer experience.

•Leveraging data analytics for personalized customer insights

Leveraging data analytics for personalized customer insights has become increasingly essential in today's business landscape. By harnessing the power of data, businesses can gain valuable insights into customer behavior, preferences, and needs, allowing them to deliver personalized experiences and enhance customer satisfaction.

Data analytics involves the collection, processing, and analysis of customer data to uncover patterns, trends, and correlations. This data can be sourced from various touchpoints such as customer interactions, purchase history, website behavior, social media engagements, and more. Through advanced analytics techniques, businesses can extract meaningful information from these data sets and translate them into actionable insights.

Personalized customer insights enable businesses to understand individual customer preferences, anticipate their needs, and tailor offerings accordingly. By analyzing data, businesses can identify customer segments, create customer profiles, and develop targeted marketing campaigns. This level of personalization enhances customer engagement, builds stronger relationships, and ultimately drives customer loyalty.

Data analytics also allows businesses to track customer interactions and touchpoints across multiple channels. By integrating data from various sources, businesses can create a holistic view of the customer journey. This comprehensive understanding helps identify pain points, optimize customer experiences, and address any gaps in service delivery.

Data analytics enables businesses to measure and track key performance indicators (KPIs) related to customer satisfaction, such as Net Promoter Score (NPS) or customer retention rate. These metrics provide insights into customer loyalty and advocacy, allowing businesses to make data-driven decisions to improve customer relationships and drive business growth.

To leverage data analytics effectively, businesses need robust data management systems and tools. This includes data collection methods, data storage, data cleaning and preparation, as well as analytical tools and techniques. Additionally, data privacy and security should be prioritized to ensure compliance with regulations and protect customer information.

Leveraging data analytics for personalized customer insights empowers businesses to understand customer behavior, preferences, and needs on an individual level. By analyzing data, businesses can deliver tailored experiences, optimize customer journeys, and build stronger relationships. This data-driven approach enhances customer satisfaction, drives customer loyalty, and ultimately contributes to business success in today's competitive marketplace.

Chapter 18: Social Media and Online Reputation Management

This chapter explores the significance of social media in today's digital landscape and its impact on a business's reputation. It delves into strategies for effectively managing online presence, building brand reputation, and engaging with customers on social platforms. The chapter emphasizes the importance of monitoring and responding to customer feedback, handling online reviews, and leveraging social media for brand building and customer engagement. It provides insights on social media best practices, reputation management tools, and tactics to maintain a positive online image. Overall, the chapter equips businesses with the knowledge to leverage social media for brand reputation management and customer satisfaction.

•Harnessing the power of social media for brand building and customer engagement

Harnessing the power of social media for brand building and customer engagement is a vital aspect of modern business strategy. With billions of active users on various social media platforms, businesses have a tremendous opportunity to reach and connect with their target audience on a global scale.

To harness the power of social media effectively, businesses must develop a comprehensive social media strategy. This involves identifying the platforms that align with their target audience and business objectives. By creating engaging and relevant content, businesses can build brand awareness, establish credibility, and foster positive associations with their brand.

One key aspect of brand building through social media is creating a consistent brand image and voice. By maintaining a cohesive brand identity across all social media channels, businesses can reinforce their brand message and values, making it easier for customers to recognize and engage with the brand.

Social media also provides a valuable platform for customer engagement. Through social media, businesses can directly interact with their audience, respond to inquiries and feedback, and provide timely customer support. By actively engaging with customers, businesses can build stronger relationships, increase customer loyalty, and gain valuable insights into customer preferences and needs.

In addition to organic engagement, social media offers various advertising and targeting options that businesses can leverage to reach their desired audience effectively. Through paid social media advertising, businesses can reach a broader audience, target specific demographics, and drive traffic to their website or online store.

Furthermore, social media analytics tools provide valuable insights into audience demographics, engagement rates, and content performance. By analyzing these metrics, businesses can refine their social media strategy, optimize their content, and make data-driven decisions to improve their brand building and customer engagement efforts.

Harnessing the power of social media for brand building and customer engagement is a dynamic and ever-evolving process. It requires a deep understanding of the target audience, effective content creation, consistent branding, proactive customer engagement, and ongoing analysis of performance metrics. By leveraging social media platforms strategically, businesses can amplify their brand reach, foster customer loyalty, and stay ahead in today's competitive digital landscape.

•Leveraging social listening for customer insights and sentiment analysis

Leveraging social listening for customer insights and sentiment analysis is a valuable practice for businesses in today's digital age. Social listening refers to the process of monitoring and analyzing online conversations and mentions of a brand, product, or industry across various social media platforms.

By actively listening to what customers are saying on social media, businesses can gain valuable insights into their preferences, needs, and opinions. Social listening allows businesses to understand customer sentiments, identify trends, and uncover opportunities for improvement. It provides a direct line of communication with customers, enabling businesses to address their concerns, answer their questions, and engage in meaningful conversations.

Through sentiment analysis, businesses can assess the overall sentiment and emotions associated with their brand or specific products and services. By analyzing the positive, negative, or neutral sentiment expressed in social media conversations, businesses can gauge customer satisfaction, identify areas of improvement, and make data-driven decisions to enhance their offerings.

Social listening and sentiment analysis also play a crucial role in reputation management. By monitoring online conversations and promptly addressing any negative sentiment or customer complaints, businesses can mitigate potential reputation risks and maintain a positive brand image. Additionally, identifying positive sentiment and user-generated content allows businesses to leverage these favorable experiences for marketing purposes and customer advocacy.

To leverage social listening effectively, businesses can employ social listening tools and platforms that enable real-time monitoring and analysis of social media conversations. These tools provide advanced features such as keyword tracking, sentiment analysis, and trend identification. By harnessing these technologies, businesses can streamline the process of social listening and gain actionable insights to inform their marketing strategies, product development, and customer engagement initiatives.

Leveraging social listening for customer insights and sentiment analysis empowers businesses to stay connected with their audience, gain a deeper understanding of customer preferences, and identify opportunities for growth and improvement. By actively monitoring and analyzing social media conversations, businesses can adapt their strategies, enhance customer experiences, and build stronger relationships with their target audience.

- Utilizing social media platforms for proactive customer support

Utilizing social media platforms for proactive customer support is a powerful strategy for businesses to provide timely assistance, build customer relationships, and enhance overall customer satisfaction. Social media platforms offer a convenient and accessible channel for customers to reach out to businesses with their queries, concerns, or feedback.

By actively monitoring social media channels, businesses can identify customer inquiries or complaints and respond promptly. Proactive customer support involves actively seeking out customer interactions and addressing them in a timely manner, rather than waiting for customers to reach out first. This approach demonstrates attentiveness and a commitment to customer satisfaction.

Social media platforms also allow businesses to engage with customers in a public forum, providing transparency and building trust. By resolving customer issues openly and transparently, businesses can showcase their commitment to customer service and potentially turn negative experiences into positive ones. Moreover, resolving customer queries or concerns publicly can also benefit other customers who may have similar questions, thereby providing a self-service knowledge base.

Social media platforms often have features like direct messaging, comments, or chatbots that facilitate instant communication with customers. Businesses can leverage these features to provide personalized and real-time support. The convenience and immediacy of social media platforms enable businesses to address customer inquiries efficiently, leading to higher customer satisfaction levels.

Social media platforms offer an opportunity for businesses to proactively engage with customers through proactive content sharing, educational posts, or helpful tips. By providing valuable information and insights related to their products or services, businesses can position themselves as trusted advisors and thought leaders in their industry. This proactive approach not only enhances the customer experience but also helps build brand loyalty and advocacy.

Chapter 19: Effective Complaint Handling and Conflict Resolution

This chapter focuses on strategies and techniques to address customer complaints and resolve conflicts in a professional and satisfactory manner. It explores the importance of actively listening to customer concerns, empathizing with their experiences, and taking appropriate actions to rectify the issues. The chapter emphasizes the significance of clear and open communication, conflict resolution skills, and problem-solving techniques to transform negative situations into positive outcomes. It provides practical guidance on handling difficult customers, managing escalated situations, and fostering positive relationships through effective complaint resolution.

- Implementing strategies for handling customer complaints and resolving conflicts

Implementing strategies for handling customer complaints and resolving conflicts is a crucial aspect of effective customer relationship management. This involves developing a systematic approach to address customer concerns, ensuring that their issues are resolved in a timely and satisfactory manner.

One key strategy is to establish clear and accessible channels for customers to voice their complaints. This can include dedicated customer support hotlines, email addresses, or online chat platforms. By providing multiple avenues for customers to reach out, businesses demonstrate their commitment to addressing concerns and maintaining open lines of communication.

When a complaint is received, it is essential to listen actively and empathetically to the customer's perspective. This involves allowing them to express their frustrations and concerns without interruption, demonstrating understanding, and validating their feelings. By acknowledging their emotions, businesses can establish a foundation of trust and show a genuine commitment to resolving the issue.

Once the complaint is understood, businesses should take prompt action to address the problem. This may involve investigating the root cause of the complaint, consulting relevant departments or individuals, and implementing corrective measures. It is important to keep the customer informed about the progress and provide realistic timelines for resolution.

In situations where conflicts arise, effective conflict resolution techniques can be employed. This includes remaining calm and composed, actively listening to all parties involved, and facilitating open and constructive dialogue. Mediation and negotiation skills can help find mutually agreeable solutions and restore positive relationships.

To ensure continuous improvement, it is essential to document and analyze customer complaints and conflict resolutions. This data can provide valuable insights into recurring issues and areas for improvement. By identifying patterns and trends, businesses can take proactive measures to prevent similar problems from occurring in the future.

Ultimately, implementing effective strategies for handling customer complaints and resolving conflicts demonstrates a commitment to customer satisfaction and strengthens the overall customer relationship. It builds trust, loyalty, and a positive reputation for the business, contributing to long-term success and growth.

•Developing a customer-centric approach to complaint resolution

Developing a customer-centric approach to complaint resolution is crucial for businesses to effectively address customer concerns and maintain strong relationships. This approach involves putting the customer at the center of the resolution process and focusing on their needs and satisfaction.

First and foremost, businesses must create a culture of empathy and understanding within their organization. This involves training employees to actively listen to customers, show genuine concern, and strive for a positive outcome. By developing empathy, employees can better connect with customers and create a supportive environment for complaint resolution.

A customer-centric approach also involves providing clear and accessible channels for customers to voice their complaints. This can include dedicated complaint hotlines, online complaint forms, or in-person meetings. By making it easy for customers to provide feedback, businesses show their commitment to addressing their concerns and improving their experience.

When a complaint is received, it is important to respond promptly and professionally. Businesses should acknowledge the complaint, thank the customer for bringing it to their attention, and assure them that their concerns will be taken seriously. Timely and personalized responses demonstrate respect for the customer and their feedback.

In the resolution process, businesses should aim for a fair and mutually beneficial outcome. This may involve investigating the issue thoroughly, consulting relevant parties, and offering appropriate solutions or compensation. The goal is to resolve the complaint in a way that satisfies the customer and restores their trust in the business.

Transparency is another key element of a customer-centric approach to complaint resolution. Businesses should keep the customer informed about the progress of the resolution, providing updates and realistic timelines. Open communication helps build trust and reassures the customer that their complaint is being taken seriously.

To ensure continuous improvement, businesses should also analyze complaint data to identify trends and patterns. This data can provide valuable insights into areas where the business can improve products, services, or processes. By addressing root causes of complaints, businesses can prevent similar issues from recurring in the future.

Developing a customer-centric approach to complaint resolution involves fostering empathy, providing accessible channels for feedback, responding promptly and professionally, aiming for fair outcomes, maintaining transparency, and using complaint data to drive continuous improvement. By prioritizing the needs and satisfaction of customers, businesses can effectively address complaints, strengthen customer relationships, and enhance their overall reputation.

•Turning negative experiences into positive outcomes through empathy and action

Turning negative experiences into positive outcomes through empathy and action is a crucial aspect of effective complaint handling and customer service. When customers encounter issues or have negative experiences, it presents an opportunity for businesses to demonstrate their commitment to customer satisfaction and turn the situation around.

Empathy plays a vital role in this process. By showing genuine understanding and concern for the customer's feelings and frustrations, businesses can create a connection and validate the customer's experience. This involves actively listening to their concerns, acknowledging their emotions, and empathizing with their perspective.

Once empathy is established, businesses must take appropriate action to address the issue. This may involve investigating the root cause of the problem, involving relevant stakeholders, and implementing solutions to prevent similar issues in the future. Prompt and effective action shows the customer that their concerns are being taken seriously and that the business is committed to resolving the situation.

In addition to resolving the immediate issue, businesses should also go above and beyond to provide additional value or compensation when appropriate. This could include offering a sincere apology, providing a refund or discount, or offering complimentary products or services. By taking proactive steps to rectify the situation and exceed customer expectations, businesses can turn a negative experience into a positive one.

Furthermore, businesses should use negative feedback as an opportunity for continuous improvement. Analyzing customer complaints and identifying trends or recurring issues can help businesses identify areas for improvement in their products, services, or processes. By addressing these issues, businesses can prevent future negative experiences and enhance overall customer satisfaction.

Overall, turning negative experiences into positive outcomes requires empathy, swift and effective action, going above and beyond to provide value, and using feedback as a catalyst for improvement. By successfully resolving customer issues and exceeding their expectations, businesses can not only retain the customer's loyalty but also enhance their reputation and build stronger customer relationships.

- Training employees in conflict management and effective communication

Training employees in conflict management and effective communication is essential for businesses to handle customer complaints and resolve conflicts in a professional and efficient manner. Conflict management training equips employees with the necessary skills and techniques to address challenging situations, diffuse tensions, and find mutually beneficial resolutions.

Effective communication is at the core of conflict management. Through training, employees learn how to actively listen to customer concerns, ask clarifying questions, and respond with empathy and understanding. They also learn how to express themselves clearly, assertively, and respectfully, avoiding misunderstandings and escalating tensions.

Conflict management training also emphasizes the importance of remaining calm and composed in challenging situations. Employees learn how to manage their emotions, respond to customer anger or frustration with empathy, and maintain a professional demeanor throughout the interaction. They are trained to focus on problem-solving and finding solutions rather than engaging in arguments or confrontations.

Additionally, conflict management training includes role-playing exercises, case studies, and simulations to simulate real-life conflict scenarios. This allows employees to practice their skills and receive feedback on their performance, enabling them to refine their conflict resolution abilities.

Effective communication training helps employees develop strong interpersonal skills, such as active listening, empathy, and non-verbal communication. They learn how to adapt their communication style to different customer personalities and situations, ensuring that their messages are clear, respectful, and well-received.

By investing in conflict management and effective communication training, businesses empower their employees to handle customer complaints and conflicts professionally, resulting in improved customer satisfaction, enhanced brand reputation, and stronger customer relationships. Employees who are equipped with these skills are better prepared to de-escalate conflicts, address customer concerns, and find mutually satisfactory resolutions, ultimately contributing to the overall success of the business.

Chapter 20: Customer-Centric Sales and Marketing Strategies

This chapter delves into the importance of aligning sales and marketing efforts with the needs and preferences of customers. It explores the strategies and approaches those businesses can adopt to create a customer-centric approach in their sales and marketing activities. This chapter highlights the significance of understanding customer motivations, tailoring marketing campaigns, and utilizing data-driven insights to drive sales. It emphasizes the importance of building strong relationships with customers, providing personalized experiences, and leveraging effective sales techniques to maximize customer satisfaction and drive business growth.

- Aligning sales and marketing efforts with customer needs and preferences

Aligning sales and marketing efforts with customer needs and preferences is essential for businesses to succeed in today's customer-centric landscape. This alignment ensures that the products or services offered meet the specific requirements of the target audience and effectively communicate their value proposition. By understanding customer needs and preferences, businesses can tailor their sales and marketing strategies to resonate with their target market.

To achieve this alignment, businesses must conduct thorough market research and gather customer insights. This involves analyzing demographic data, conducting surveys, and leveraging customer feedback to gain a deep understanding of what customers truly want and need. By identifying customer pain points, challenges, and motivations, businesses can align their sales and marketing efforts accordingly.

Once customer needs and preferences are identified, businesses can develop targeted marketing campaigns and messages that address these specific requirements. This includes creating compelling content, utilizing appropriate communication channels, and employing persuasive techniques that resonate with the target audience. By focusing on customer-centric messaging, businesses can effectively engage customers and differentiate themselves from the competition.

Aligning sales and marketing efforts involves coordinating activities between these two departments. Collaboration and communication are key in ensuring that marketing efforts generate qualified leads that sales teams can effectively convert into customers. By sharing customer insights, feedback, and market trends, sales and marketing teams can work together to develop strategies that optimize customer engagement and drive conversions.

Technology plays a crucial role in aligning sales and marketing efforts with customer needs and preferences. Customer relationship management (CRM) systems and marketing automation tools provide valuable insights and data, enabling businesses to track customer interactions, preferences, and behaviors. This data-driven approach allows businesses to personalize their sales and marketing efforts, delivering relevant messages and offers at the right time and through the preferred channels.

Aligning sales and marketing efforts with customer needs and preferences allows businesses to build stronger relationships, enhance customer satisfaction, and drive business growth. By understanding and addressing customer needs, businesses can create a seamless and tailored customer experience that resonates with their target audience and ultimately leads to increased sales and customer loyalty.

•Developing targeted and personalized marketing campaigns

Developing targeted and personalized marketing campaigns is a strategic approach that enables businesses to connect with their audience on a deeper level and increase the effectiveness of their marketing efforts. By tailoring messages and offers to specific customer segments, businesses can deliver highly relevant and engaging content that resonates with individual preferences and needs.

To develop targeted and personalized marketing campaigns, businesses need to start by understanding their target audience. This involves conducting thorough market research, analyzing customer data, and segmenting the audience based on demographic, psychographic, and behavioral characteristics. By identifying specific customer segments, businesses can tailor their marketing messages to resonate with each group.

Once the target audience is identified, businesses can craft tailored messages that speak directly to the needs and pain points of each segment. This may involve highlighting specific benefits, addressing common challenges, or presenting solutions that align with their interests. Personalized campaigns also leverage data and technology to deliver content and offers that are relevant to each individual customer, based on their past behavior, preferences, or demographics.

Effective targeting and personalization require a deep understanding of customer behavior and preferences. Businesses can leverage customer data, such as purchase history, website interactions, and social media engagement, to gain insights into individual preferences and interests. This data-driven approach allows businesses to create highly relevant and personalized marketing campaigns that resonate with customers on a personal level.

Technology plays a crucial role in enabling targeted and personalized marketing campaigns. Customer relationship management (CRM) systems, marketing automation tools, and data analytics platforms provide businesses with the necessary tools to collect, analyze, and leverage customer data. These tools enable businesses to segment their audience, create personalized content, automate marketing workflows, and measure campaign effectiveness.

By developing targeted and personalized marketing campaigns, businesses can enhance customer engagement, improve conversion rates, and foster long-term customer loyalty. These campaigns demonstrate that businesses understand their customers' unique needs and are committed to delivering relevant and valuable experiences. In turn, customers are more likely to respond positively to these campaigns, resulting in increased brand loyalty and ultimately driving business growth.

●Utilizing customer data for more effective lead generation and nurturing

Utilizing customer data for more effective lead generation and nurturing is a critical aspect of modern marketing strategies. By leveraging the insights gained from customer data, businesses can identify and target potential customers more accurately, resulting in higher quality leads and improved conversion rates.

One way to utilize customer data for lead generation is by analyzing past customer behavior and purchase patterns. By studying customer interactions with the business, such as website visits, product purchases, or engagement with marketing campaigns, businesses can identify key indicators of potential interest. This information can be used to develop targeted marketing campaigns and personalized messaging to capture the attention of potential customers and generate leads.

Customer data can also be used to refine and optimize lead nurturing strategies. By understanding customer preferences, pain points, and purchase triggers, businesses can create tailored content and experiences that guide leads through the sales funnel. This might involve sending personalized emails, offering relevant content or promotions, or engaging with leads on social media platforms. The goal is to deliver value to leads at each stage of their buyer's journey, building trust and increasing the likelihood of conversion.

Customer data can help businesses identify potential upsell and cross-sell opportunities. By analyzing purchase history and customer preferences, businesses can identify complementary products or services that may be of interest to existing customers. This allows businesses to proactively engage with customers and present relevant upselling or cross-selling offers, driving additional revenue and enhancing customer satisfaction.

To effectively utilize customer data for lead generation and nurturing, businesses need robust data management and analysis systems. Customer relationship management (CRM) platforms, marketing automation tools, and data analytics software can provide the necessary infrastructure to collect, organize, and analyze customer data. These systems enable businesses to segment their target audience, personalize marketing campaigns, track customer interactions, and measure the effectiveness of lead generation efforts.

By leveraging customer data for more effective lead generation and nurturing, businesses can optimize their marketing strategies, increase lead quality, and improve overall conversion rates. This approach allows businesses to focus their efforts on the most promising leads, deliver personalized and relevant content, and ultimately drive business growth and profitability.

•Building strong relationships with prospects and customers through effective sales techniques

Building strong relationships with prospects and customers is crucial for successful sales outcomes and long-term business growth. Effective sales techniques play a key role in establishing and nurturing these relationships, ensuring that customers feel valued, understood, and supported throughout the sales process.

One important aspect of building strong relationships is active listening. Sales professionals must attentively listen to prospects and customers to understand their needs, pain points, and goals. By actively listening, salespeople can uncover valuable insights and tailor their approach to address specific customer challenges. This helps to build trust and rapport, demonstrating to customers that their concerns are genuinely heard and understood.

In addition to listening, effective communication is essential. Sales professionals should articulate the value proposition of their products or services clearly and concisely, ensuring that customers grasp how their needs will be met or problems solved. They should adapt their communication style to resonate with different individuals and organizations, adjusting the level of technical detail or business impact as needed.

Building strong relationships also involves providing

exceptional customer service. Sales professionals should be responsive, reliable, and proactive in addressing customer inquiries, concerns, or requests. Timely follow-ups and regular communication demonstrate commitment and build confidence in the customer-salesperson relationship.

Another crucial aspect of effective sales techniques is building credibility and trust. Sales professionals should showcase their expertise and industry knowledge, positioning themselves as trusted advisors rather than mere salespeople. By providing valuable insights, relevant information, and personalized recommendations, sales professionals can establish themselves as partners in the customer's success.

To truly build strong relationships, sales professionals should adopt a long-term perspective. They should focus not only on closing individual sales but also on nurturing ongoing customer relationships. This involves regular check-ins, seeking feedback, and offering continuous support to ensure customer satisfaction and loyalty.

Furthermore, effective sales techniques incorporate relationship-building strategies such as networking, referrals, and testimonials. Sales professionals can leverage existing customer relationships to expand their network and acquire new leads. Happy customers can become advocates, referring their contacts and sharing positive experiences to attract new business.

By employing effective sales techniques, sales professionals can build strong and mutually beneficial relationships with prospects and customers. These relationships are the foundation for repeat business, customer loyalty, and positive word-of-mouth referrals, ultimately driving revenue growth and business success.

key takeaways

- Understanding the importance of customer relationships in driving business success
- Recognizing the impact of positive customer experiences on loyalty and advocacy
- Building a customer-centric organizational culture
- Understanding and meeting customer needs and expectations
- Mapping the customer journey to identify touchpoints and interactions
- Developing effective customer communication strategies
- Delivering exceptional customer experiences through personalization and customization
- Building trust and loyalty through reliable and consistent service
- Implementing customer success strategies for long-term growth
- Fostering a customer-centric culture throughout the organization
- Leveraging technology and data for enhanced customer interactions
- Managing customer expectations and resolving conflicts effectively
- Implementing effective complaint handling and conflict resolution strategies

- Aligning sales and marketing efforts with customer needs and preferences
- Leveraging customer feedback for continuous improvement
- Building strong relationships with prospects and customers through effective sales techniques
- Monitoring and managing online reputation and customer reviews
- Embracing innovation and adaptability in customer service
- Utilizing social media and technology for customer engagement and support
- Measuring customer satisfaction and loyalty through key metrics

What organizations generally miss

There can be several reasons why organization may not be able to serve customers effectively. Some common reasons include:

Lack of understanding of customer needs: If a company doesn't have a clear understanding of its target customers and their needs, it becomes difficult to meet their expectations.

Inadequate customer service training: If employees are not properly trained in customer service skills, they may struggle to effectively address customer inquiries, resolve issues, and provide a positive experience.

Poor communication channels: If the company lacks efficient communication channels, such as a responsive customer support system or easy-to-use online platforms, it can lead to delays and frustrations in customer interactions.

Inconsistent service quality: If there is inconsistency in delivering quality service across different customer touchpoints, it can erode customer trust and satisfaction.

Lack of empowerment for customer-facing employees: If frontline employees do not have the authority or resources to make decisions and resolve customer issues independently, it can hinder the company's ability to provide satisfactory service.

Insufficient feedback and evaluation processes: Without effective feedback mechanisms and regular evaluation of customer interactions, a company may struggle to identify areas for improvement and address customer concerns.

Failure to adapt to changing customer expectations: If a company doesn't keep up with evolving customer expectations and industry trends, it can result in outdated products, services, or processes that no longer meet customer needs.

Lack of customer-centric culture: If the company does not prioritize customer-centricity and fails to instill a customer-focused mindset across all levels of the organization, it can hinder the ability to consistently deliver excellent service.

Lack of personalization: If the company fails to personalize its interactions and offerings based on individual customer preferences and needs, it may struggle to build strong connections and deliver relevant solutions.

Complex and cumbersome processes: If the company's processes for ordering, returns, or issue resolution are overly complex or time-consuming, it can lead to customer dissatisfaction and potential churn.

Poor internal communication: If there are communication gaps within the company, such as between different departments or teams, it can lead to misalignment and negatively impact the customer experience.

It's important for organization to address these challenges and invest in strategies and practices that prioritize customer satisfaction and success.

What not to do

Certainly! Here are some key points of what not to do to maintain good customer relations:

Neglecting customer complaints: Ignoring or dismissing customer complaints can lead to dissatisfaction and a negative perception of your brand.

Lack of responsiveness: Failing to respond promptly to customer inquiries or issues can leave customers feeling unimportant and uncared for.

Poor communication: Communication breakdowns, such as not listening attentively to customers or providing unclear information, can lead to frustration and misunderstandings.

Being unprofessional or rude: Displaying unprofessional behavior or treating customers disrespectfully can severely damage your relationship with them.

Overpromising and underdelivering: Setting unrealistic expectations and failing to meet them can result in disappointment and loss of trust.

Lack of empathy: Failing to understand and empathize with customers' needs and concerns can make them feel undervalued and unimportant.

Neglecting customer feedback: Disregarding customer feedback or failing to act upon it can create the perception that their opinions don't matter.

Inconsistency in service: Providing inconsistent service experiences across different channels or touchpoints can lead to confusion and frustration.

Lack of personalization: Treating customers as generic entities rather than addressing their individual needs and preferences can diminish the customer experience.

Poor problem resolution: Mishandling customer issues or providing inadequate solutions can damage trust and leave customers unsatisfied.

Neglecting to appreciate loyal customers: Failing to recognize and reward loyal customers can make them feel unappreciated and drive them to seek alternatives.

By avoiding these common pitfalls, businesses can improve customer relations, enhance customer satisfaction, and foster long-term loyalty.

Epilogue

We have explored the essential strategies, principles, and practices that form the foundation of building strong and successful customer relationships. We have delved into the importance of understanding customer needs, delivering exceptional experiences, and fostering trust and loyalty. Throughout the chapters, we have emphasized the significance of customer-centricity and the power of effective communication, personalization, and continuous improvement.

As we conclude this journey, it is important to remember that creating and maintaining positive customer relationships is an ongoing process. It requires dedication, empathy, and a genuine commitment to meeting customer expectations. By implementing the insights and strategies shared in this book, businesses can navigate the complex landscape of customer relations with confidence and achieve remarkable results.

Let us remember that customers are the lifeblood of any organization, and by prioritizing their needs, delivering exceptional experiences, and continuously striving to exceed their expectations, we can build enduring relationships that drive business growth and success. May this book serve as a guide and inspiration to forge meaningful connections with customers and embark on a path of customer-centric excellence.

Thank You

www.ingramcontent.com/pod-product-compliance
Lightning Source LLC
Chambersburg PA
CBHW070924260726
48661CB00003B/821

9798857759691